RUSSIA AT WAR 1941-45

RUSSIA AT WAR
1941-45

Introduction by
Vladimir Karpov

Preface by Harrison Salisbury

With text by
Georgii Drozdov and Evgenii Ryabko
translated by Lydia Kmetyuk

Edited by Carey Schofield

GUILD PUBLISHING LONDON

This edition published 1988 by Guild Publishing by arrangement with
Century Hutchinson Ltd, Brookmount House, 62–65 Chandos Place, London WC2N 4NW

This book was designed and produced by
JOHN CALMANN AND KING LTD, LONDON
in association with Alexandria Press Ltd.

Designer Robert Updegraff
Phototypeset by Wyvern Typesetting Ltd, Bristol
Printed in Singapore by Toppan Ltd

Title-page: *Kerch. Relatives try to identify the dead after the Germans have massacred all the men in a village. This is one of the most famous photographs taken during the war in Russia. It was at Kerch that the Russians received their evidence of large-scale Nazi atrocities. Several thousand Jews and others had been shot and buried in huge trenches outside the town.*

Contents

Acknowledgements

This publication has been prepared in collaboration with the USSR Commission for UNESCO.
The Editor would like to thank the staff of VAAP, the Copyright Agency of the USSR, for their help with the preparation of this book. A particular debt of gratitude is owed to Ludmilla Smirnova, Alexander Meledin and Alexander Melikov, without whose kindness and patience the task would have been infinitely more difficult. Grateful acknowledgement is also due to Sergei Klockov of the USSR Commission for UNESCO for continual help and support throughout the project, and to Terry Charman of the Imperial War Museum, London, for his advice.

The excerpts in the book are taken from the following sources:

p. 25   Sergei Gvazov, from an interview with the authors, Kiev, 1975.

p. 29   Georgii Bekasov, in *Recollections of the War Years*, edited by A. Sprigis. Liyesma Publishing House, Riga, 1960.

p. 34   Yaroslav Branko, from an interview with the authors, Lvov, 1975.

p. 37   *The Sacred War*: Lyrics – V. I. Lebdyev-Kumach
        Music – A. V. Alexandrov

p. 41   Georgii Namzaev, from an interview with the authors, Kharkov, 1975.

p. 51   Sergeant Ivan Sahov, from an interview with the authors, Gorky, 1974.

p. 53   Igor Butoma, in *1,418 Days*, edited by V. Khutsishvili. Sakartvelo Publishers, Tbilisi, 1975.

p. 62   Nushi Dudoeva, from an interview in the Soviet television programme, *Brotherhood*, 1974.

p. 65   Anastasia Yeremenko, in *The Trains go off to the East*, edited by I. Naimov. Nayka, Moscow, 1966.

p. 66   Georgii Gogoberidze in *Exploits of the Rearguard*, edited by L. Glebova. Politizdat, Moscow, 1970.

p. 71   Dmitri Shostakovich, in *Pravda*, 29 March 1942.

p. 73   Anna Zavaly, from an interview with the authors, Donetsk, 1975.

p. 74   Chodar Yenukidze, in *1,418 Days*, edited by V. Khutsishvili, Sakartvelo Publishers, Tbilisi, 1975.

p. 77   Mikhail Dorofeev, in *The Trains go off to the East*, edited by I. Naimov, Nayka, Moscow, 1966.

p. 79   Katerina Yelina, from an interview in the Soviet television programme *Mail about the Action from the Front*, 1980.

p. 101 Leonid Panteleev, in *Living Memories*, Lenizdat, Leningrad, 1966.

p. 106 Ivan Maximov, in *A Memory*, edited by A. Varsobin, Lenizdat, Leningrad, 1985.

p. 107 Leonid Panteleev, in *Living Memories*, Lenizdat, Leningrad, 1966.

p. 108 Georgi Kulagin, from his diary in the City Museum, Leningrad.

p. 124 Pantelei Kondratyev, from an interview in the television film, *Brotherhood*, 1974.

p. 126 Mikhail Gusev, from his journal in the archives of the Museum of the Soviet Army.

p. 129 Sergeant Grigorii Nikolski, from his letter in the archives of the Museum of the Soviet Army.

p. 147 Nina Zaretskaya, in *In Occupied Territory* by Vladimir Yakorenko, Politizdat, Moscow, 1966.

p. 148 Mikhail Naumov, in *The Partisans' True Stories*, Molod, Kiev, 1965.

p. 151 Konstantin Zaslonov, in *Dead Heroes Speak*, edited by V. Kondratyev, Politizdat, Moscow, 1966.

p. 164 Lieutenant-General Rotmistrov, in 'The Speed of Attack of a Tank Army', in *Voyenno-istoricheskiy Zhurnal*, 1964.

p. 167 Ivan Boloto, from an interview with the authors, Kharkov, 1975.

p. 170 Igor Balabanov, in *In the Heat of the Kursk Battle*, edited by T. Sorokin. Kursk Book Publishing House, 1963.

p. 177 Vladimir Farberov, from an interview with the authors, Odessa, 1974.

p. 188 Olga Bykova, in *For the Sake of Life on Earth*, edited by O. Novikova, Voronezh Publishing House, Voronezh, 1970.

p. 189 Hamid Samatov, from an interview with the authors, Tashkent, 1974.

p. 195 Katerina Bochkariova, from an interview with the authors, Sebastopol, 1975.

p. 201 Alexander Guskov, in *Frontline Reportage of the War*, edited by Y. Yurov, Politizdat, Moscow, 1970.

p. 205 Yefim Golbreich, in *On War, Comrades and Myself*, edited by R. Kovalenko, Politizdat, Moscow, 1970.

p. 207 Leonid Sosnin, from an interview with the authors, Rostov-on-the-Don, 1975.

p. 210 Vladimir Farberov, from an interview with the authors, Odessa, 1974.

p. 211 Alexander Pankov, in *1,418 Days*, edited by V. Khutsishvili, Sakartvelo Publishers, Tbilisi, 1975.

p. 212 Mikhail Sholokhov, in *Along the Road to the Front*, The Young Guard Publishing House, Moscow, 1965.

p. 213 Vladimir Farberov, from an interview with the authors, Odessa, 1974.

p. 216 Boris Shugayev, from an interview with the authors, Minsk, 1975.

p. 217 Ivan Kiryanov, from his letter in the archives of the Museum of the Soviet Army.

p. 218 *Ah, those roads . . .*: Lyrics – Lev Oshanin
        Music – Anatoli Novikov

p. 226 Vladimir Zhogov, from an interview in the Soviet television programme *Mail about the Action from the Front*, 1980.

p. 233 Nikolai Redkoborodov, in *Pravda*, 24 July 1970.

p. 234 Valentina Tokaryeva, from an interview with the authors, Minsk, 1975.

p. 240 Glafira Ter-Akopova in *1,418 Days*, edited by V. Khutsishvili, Sakartvelo Publishers, Tbilisi, 1975.

p. 243 Georgii Zhukov, in *Reminiscences and Reflections*, published by Novosti, Moscow, 1969.

Preface

I know of no one who was alive in Russia on 22nd June 1941 who does not remember that summer day, the solstice, longest day of the year, a day when in Leningrad night does not fall, a day in most of Russia when there is only a brief twilight and then the sun rises anew.

But in Russia they remember 22nd June not for the soft breezes, the endless evening, the slow saunter of boys and girls, the haunting songs of young voices and the play of the accordion, the lazy strolls of couples, arms entwined, in the parks of Moscow and Kiev. They remember it as a day of horror, the day the Nazis struck (so it seemed) out of a clear sky, attacking the Soviet Union. It was the start of the greatest, most terrible war of modern times, Hitler against Stalin.

Between 22nd June 1941 and 9th May 1945, when the Germans finally surrendered, the great city of Leningrad suffered through the longest siege of contemporary history. The most stubborn and bloody battle of our day – critical to the fate of Russia and the world – had been fought and won by the Russians at Stalingrad. A titanic struggle of tanks and armour, the like of which has never been seen, was fought (and is hardly known in the West) at Kursk-Orel, breaking Hitler's armoured back. Never again would the Wehrmacht mount a massive offensive.

Within the compass of the four years after 22nd June many millions of Soviet lives would be lost, in one way or another, on the battlefield or within the civilian population. The figures are too large for our minds to grasp. But a simple fact brings them home to us. I do not know a single Russian family which did not suffer the loss of a father, a son, a brother and often many more. Many Russians I met in wartime – and after the war – were the sole survivors of their family and many families were wiped out to the last member.

We Americans, thank God, have never fought a war like that; not even our bloody Civil War when brother fought brother took that kind of toll. Russia lost over ten per cent of its population either in combat or indirectly. To this day the word 'war' means something different to a Russian than it does to Americans or even the British.

We do not yet, forty years later, know the full story. Mikhail Gorbachev's *glasnost* has cast a beam of light into some dark corners but there is much we still do not know of the story of Russia's war and the life of her people. The pictures in this book, many only now released from the archives, give us much insight of what war meant to the men and women who lived through it – and those who did not – on the Eastern Front. A rush of new historical detail is beginning to flesh out the picture of how much responsibility for this great tragedy must be laid on the shoulders of the Soviet leader, Josef Stalin.

Hitler's attack on Russia on 22nd June was accomplished with complete surprise. The Russian people were going about their ordinary lives unaware that danger was at hand. True, a few steps had been taken to reinforce Soviet garrisons at the border, but only in the last days, and the public knew nothing of this. Most of the reinforcements were still in transit and those who had arrived at the frontiers had no proper fortifications. They were overrun in the first hours. The air

The Red Army had a number of cavalry units during World War II, the best known of which were General Belov's Corps and General Plyev's Corps. Each 'Front' (Army Group) had two or three divisions of cavalry which it used to protect flanks and for operating over difficult terrain.

In the first months of the war, cavalry units carried out raids into occupied territory. Later on they were used together with tanks, when the Soviet offensive began. But during the spring of 1944 they came into their own, because horses could cope with deep mud better than any vehicle.

In 1943 there were 41 cavalry divisions, 600,000 men altogether. By the end of the war there were 34 divisions.

force, contrary to western intelligence, was very powerful but it was virtually wiped out on the ground by noon of 22nd June. Before the day was over the Nazis had smashed the forward elements of the Russians so badly that in the evening Moscow GHQ could not even raise the commanders on the hot line to find out what was happening. Stalin himself had fled the Kremlin and gone into seclusion at his country villa, certain that all was lost, leaving his associates to cope with the disaster.

None of this need have been. No man in the world had more advance notice. Stalin's extraordinary intelligence service had been warning for months of the Nazi preparations. His No. 1 spy Richard Sorge, in Tokyo, had given Stalin precise day and date of the Nazi attack, the German order of battle and the points of main assault. Prime Minister Winston Churchill had warned Stalin. Franklin D. Roosevelt warned Stalin. Even Mao Zedong in faraway Yanan in China's northern Shaanxi province warned him. Stalin's generals tried to tell him but Stalin would not listen. He insisted it was all a trick. Hitler wanted to provoke the Russians into giving him a cause for attack. Or Churchill was trying to embroil Russia in war with Hitler.

Not until the evening of 20th June did the signals become so alarming that Stalin began to pay some heed. All the following Saturday, 21st June, his Foreign Minister Molotov tried to get in touch with Hitler or von Ribbentrop in Berlin. No luck. No one answered the phone. Stalin sent cautious word on Saturday night to commanders to be on the alert – but not to provoke Hitler.

The messages came too late. The Nazi attackers were already pouring over the Soviet borders. As for the Soviet people, not until Molotov made his unexpected broadcast at noon on Sunday did they know they were at war. Since 3 or 4 am German war planes had been bombing their western cities and German tanks had been blasting through the border defences into open country.

The first six months of war was unrelieved tragedy. The Germans smashed into the Ukraine, surrounding Soviet armies in an enormous enclave. By the time they drew the noose around Kiev they had killed or captured 200,000 troops. The whole of Russia's breadbasket, the rich Ukrainian farmland, was overrun. Hitler reached the outskirts of Leningrad and cut the city off on 8th September from its connections with the rest of Russian land. Only Lake Ladoga afforded access to the city where 3,100,000 people were blockaded. By October Leningraders began to die of hunger. By winter the death rate was thousands a day. How any human could survive I cannot understand today, any more than I did when I first set foot in the city a few days after the siege was lifted on 26th January 1944.

Leningraders had no heat. They had only a crust of bread a day. Every water-pipe froze. Every drop had to be carried in icy pails from the Neva river. There was no transport. No streetcars. No automobiles. No gas. No lights. Newspapers halted. Only a flickering radio carried on. People starved and froze to death in their apartments. By the end of winter 1941–42 the frozen bodies piled up in small mountains around the cemeteries, carried there by weak and starving people on children's sleds. But Leningrad did not surrender.

The Germans rolled into the suburbs of Moscow in early October 1941. They prepared for a victory banquet in the Kremlin, but they never made it. They were halted at the gates. When I got to Moscow in 1944 I saw a burnt-out Nazi tank beside the Leningrad chausse at the Khimki river station on the outskirts. It was the high-water mark of the German offensive. The Russians in December began the long drive back, but not without more disasters. In the summer of 1942 Nazi tanks broke through onto the southern steppes and hurtled to the banks of the Volga. But they were halted at Stalingrad, which became a symbol of the stubborn courage of the Red Army and the Soviet people. They fought street by street, building by building, floor by floor and

An anti-tank gun crew takes aim, firing straight at a tank. These guns, 76.2mm field guns, model 1939 (76–39), were normally used against targets 10 or 15 kilometres (6 or 10 miles) away. During the battle of Kursk, the enemy tanks were often only 200 or 300 metres (650–950 ft) from the guns. In several cases shells destroyed the gun's sight, so the crew had to take aim by peering through the barrel.

9

finally room by room. When it was over the Russians had won. General Paulus and 300,000 German soldiers surrendered. With that victory the world knew that Hitler was finished; that Russia and her allies, the United States and Britain, would win.

The war would go on more than two years. More hundreds of thousands of Russian lives would be expended. But step by step the blood-soaked soil would be regained. The Wehrmacht fought every foot of the way but with the American and British landing on the Normandy beaches on 6th June 1944 the pressure became inexorable. The Soviet army entered Poland in early summer 1944 and drove into the Balkans, liberating Rumania, Bulgaria, and Czechoslovakia and helping Tito in Yugoslavia. By spring 1945 the Red Army was pushing into Austria and stood in the eastern marches of the Third Reich.

In the west the Americans and British plunged through France to the western fringes of Germany. Hitler, in madness, fought on. Only after the Red Army entered the smashed and torn city of Berlin and pounded to its very centre did he take his own life in the Reichs-chancellery bunker from which he directed the last stand. Soviet troops found the bodies of Hitler, his mistress Eva Braun, and Goebbels.

Russia at War is a record of the Russian people fighting for their existence as seen from the Soviet point of view. It is a record not familiar to many Westerners. To us the Eastern Front is an almost forgotten chapter in World War II but in Soviet memory it glows deep and inescapable, the victory over Hitler paid for in the blood of Russian men, women and children, in the destruction of Russian cities and the devastation of the countryside. It is not a forgotten war.

A Soviet machine-gun crew in action in heavy fighting in Germany.

A woman pilot being congratulated on having successfully completed a night raid. She is a member of the Tamanski Guards Air Corps Regiment, which consisted entirely of women. They were all volunteers, most of whom had learned to fly as a hobby before the war. They were described by the Germans as the 'Night Witches'.

It is traditional in the Russian army to name units after areas in which they have distinguished themselves. This meant, of course, that there were several units with the same name. These flyers had served in the Taman Peninsula. There was also a Tamanski Mechanized Division.

This book pays tribute to the Soviet generals, to Zhukov, Koniev, Chuikov and the others and even to Stalin, so mistaken before the war and in its earlier stages. But in a larger sense it is a monument in words and pictures to the ordinary Russian men and women, to all the peoples of the Soviet Union, the plain citizens whose sacrifices made victory possible.

In the Kremlin on 24th May 1945, in the presence of his great commanders, Stalin hailed the Russian people over all the others in the Soviet Union. Another people, he said, might have turned against their government in its hour of peril but 'the Russian people did not do that . . . and made the sacrifices which made certain the defeat of Germany.'

The memory of those sacrifices may burn only dimly today outside Russia but this volume and its remarkable photographs, many shown here for the first time, should light a candle whose flame will long illuminate our consciousness.

HARRISON E. SALISBURY

Introduction

More than forty years have elapsed since the last bomb, last shell and last bullet cut short the life of the last soldier in the closing battles of World War II.

For four decades Europe has been living in peace. Is that a long time? In the none too distant past the average life expectancy in Europe was forty. Today I am over sixty.

The most important event in the life of my generation was the war. We could be expected to mourn a youth wasted on battles, and sorrow and tragedy. But we don't. We all look back without regret on our grim wartime youth when we were defending our country, because there, in the front lines, each of us was indispensable. There was no one to take our place. The knowledge that we and we alone could defend our country, that on this little strip of land the Soviet Union's fate rested in our hands, filled us with pride and a sense of grave responsibility.

The Nazis intended to overcome us in six weeks. In the early stages of the war they even believed they would succeed. They took Minsk in less than a week. By August they had thrust close to Leningrad, and in November they were at Moscow. But Leningrad did not fall. Neither did Moscow. Neither did Stalingrad. It was Berlin that fell and it was in Berlin that on 8th May 1945 Germany signed the Unconditional Surrender.

Many times I had beaten back the attacks of intoxicated Nazi soldiers. They were not merely under the influence of Schnapps – they had come to our land drunk on the easy victories they had won in Europe. I am not speaking of death in the field – there are no wars without casualties. What I mean is the noncombatants, the old folk, the women and the children, the innocent people they hanged and shot. We clearly understood that this was no ordinary war. It was not territory that was being contested, but the right to live, to breathe, to speak our language, to raise our children, the right to human dignity.

I started out in the lines as a private. The wartime newsreels usually showed tanks speeding ahead in clouds of smoke and dust, or planes flying and shooting in the sky. The dark specks down below on the ground were the attacking infantry. Well, I was one of those tiny specks and I was nineteen years old then (1941). I was in action till the last day of the war. In 1942, I joined Army Reconnaissance and was promoted first to sergeant, then to lieutenant. After that, I stopped being even a speck on the screen, because scouts usually operate under cover of darkness. A group of us would penetrate the enemy lines to capture what we called a 'tongue', a prisoner who supplied information on enemy dispositions. Being a scout is a high-risk job and I was wounded three times and decorated many times for bravery.

Among the documents we captured in the enemy rear were many photographs. The Germans liked to take snapshots standing near the Eiffel Tower and the Acropolis. They even took snapshots of gallows and of women being shot in flaming villages. Some of these photographs are reproduced in this book.

War is not just an unending sequence of danger, death and thoughts of death. If it were, no one could have stood the strain even for a month, let alone four years. Side by side with danger and difficulty there were moments of rest, fun and jokes and love. So it is only natural that the troops' day-to-day life features prominently in this book alongside the horrors.

A short rest during battle. There was no phoney war on the Soviet front – from the moment of the invasion the fighting was constant.

There was a lot of work for the soldier in the war. He dug trenches and ditches, laid mines and defused them, built bridges across rivers, hauled ammunition, cooked food, washed underwear, repaired tanks, serviced planes and did a thousand other chores that all too often go unnoticed, but are indispensable. There were times when a soldier was so exhausted he was sure he would never get up again. He would fall asleep instantly, and in the morning, or even a few minutes later, if there was an alert, he'd be up and at it again, rather to his own amazement.

Never in my life have I worked with such utter physical exertion as I did during those years at the front. At the same time, never since have I felt so strong and fit. I have noticed the same in others. People seldom fell ill at the front. Even the wounded tried to get out of hospital as soon as possible, so they could return to the lines.

They say that everyone who has seen action has a battle that was especially memorable. I am no exception. When the battle I want to tell you about was being planned at headquarters, no doubt a hundred versions were contemplated. But as it happens all too often during a war, it was played out according to the hundred and first version, which no one had foreseen.

I was not present at the planning, of course, but when we received orders in the evening that the attack was to be launched under cover of darkness I realized it was to be a New Year's surprise for the fascists. The command had decided on a surprise attack to get the enemy out of their well-appointed dugouts and trenches so that they would have a chance to see what the Russian frosts are like out in the open fields.

Well, we got them out of the first line of defences, but they laid on such a wall of machine-gun and artillery fire before the second line that we had to hug the earth.

I glanced at my watch – it was 11.20 pm. I wondered if I'd live to see 1943. I was clinging to the side of a freshly made shell-hole which was slowly filling with water – it was a swampy area. When the hole filled up I'd have to get out under those bullets. That icy water was not for me.

Half an hour until the New Year. Somewhere far away people were celebrating, exchanging good wishes. I had no one beside me whom I could wish a Happy New Year. I remembered the tradition that a wish made on New Year's Eve was sure to come true. I hope I stay alive, I thought. But at the same moment I realized everyone was making the same wish, on both sides. So that was a lot of nonsense. I ought to wish for something more realistic . . . that we should take the second line of defences? But we'd do that anyway, if not today, then tomorrow. . . . So what could I wish for? College? To live to my wedding day? Whatever I thought of hinged on victory . . . then and only then could happiness become a reality.

Suppose we do win, I kept on thinking, what would I like to start my postwar life with? This may sound childish, but my dream was to return to my home town, Tashkent, where Mother, Father and, naturally, 'she' were waiting, and after the first hectic moments of greeting, I wanted to be left alone, to walk in the hush of evening down the centre of Pushkin Street, alone under the street-lamps, and I wanted the pavements to be crowded with girls in light summer frocks and boys in well-pressed trousers.

A mortar bomb landed nearby, showering me with earth and splinters. Involuntarily, I pulled in my head and looked down. At that moment I discovered another world at the bottom of the shell-hole. The circle of water looked like a transparent lens. In it, I saw what I had been dreaming of – a peaceful fathomless sky, a moon, bright stars and gossamer clouds. Then I saw a dark spectre staring out at me. Although I realized that it was my own face, I was terrified. Was the apparition an omen that I would die?

I moved warily to take a closer look, to see if the face in the mirror of water were dead or alive. That instant I felt my hair standing on end and the blood in my veins turning to ice, for in the water I saw reflected a German helmet. He was peering into the shell-hole and took me for a corpse, because I was lying in an unnatural posture, head down. I shot first and didn't miss. I leaped out of the shell-hole to see if there were any more coming. After firing a few rounds I was again forced back into the hole by the heavy fire. I looked at my watch: we were five minutes into the New Year. My fortune-telling had almost come true. In another second I would have been a corpse, very much like the one that had peered out from under the water.

My fear was turning to exhilaration. Not a bad New Year's Day present – to be alive! I looked at the body of my enemy. Who was he? He must have been someone before I killed him. Was he wishing he'd stay alive just a few minutes ago, was he wishing he'd return to his Gretchen? One thing I was sure of: he had not been thinking of death. And that was his mistake. Anyone who steps on our soil as an enemy and plunderer should, above all, think of death. I do not know who that dead soldier was, but I would like to cite three letters that did not reach their destination in Germany due to the counter-offensive launched by the Red Army at Moscow in 1941.

1st December 1941

We are now at a distance of 30 kilometres from Moscow and can see some of its spires. Soon we will have surrounded Moscow and then we'll be billeted in sumptuous winter quarters and I will send you presents which will make Aunt Minna green with envy.

K SIMANN, SS: *excerpt from a letter to his wife in Munich*

3rd December 1941

When you receive this letter the Russians will be defeated and we will be in Moscow parading in Red Square. I never dreamed I'd see so many countries. I also hope to be on hand when our troops parade in England . . .

CHRISTIAN HOELZER, SS: *excerpt from a letter to Georg Hoelzer, Altergrünau*

6th December 1941

My dear wife,

    This is hell. The Russians don't want to leave Moscow. They've launched an offensive. Every hour brings news of terrifying developments. It's so cold my very soul is freezing. It's death to venture out in the evening. I beg of you – stop writing about the silks and rubber boots I'm supposed to bring you from Moscow. Can't you understand I'm dying? I'll die for sure. I feel it.

ADOLF FORTHEIMER: *excerpt from a letter*

The field kitchen was often a kilometre or more from the front. So somebody would have to crawl, under enemy fire, to take the food to the trenches. The metal thermos in the photograph held enough food for an entire platoon: 36 to 40 men and one officer.

A soldier with an old woman in a newly liberated village near Moscow. The village had probably been occupied for about two months.

Those letters were written a mere six months after the war had started. Stalingrad still lay ahead, and the battle of Kursk. There were still three and a half years of the war to go.

From the very start we believed in victory, we believed the enemy would be defeated and we would win. Our soldiers wrote letters, too. You will find some of them in this book. People do not lie when bullets whistle overhead, they do not juggle with words and forms to express their thoughts. The men at the front knew that they would not all survive, that every letter might be the last. They wrote during intervals in the fighting, in trenches and dugouts and during short halts on marches. People at home waited desperately for news. All too often the correspondence broke off forever, and the last sad message they received said: '. . . fell gallantly in action . . .'

More than twenty million Soviet people died fighting the Nazis, forty per cent of the total death toll of World War II. Let this book remind people of the tragic past when mankind had to sacrifice fifty million people to regain freedom. Let it convey to our contemporaries, our children and grandchildren, what war is all about.

A man's memory ends with his life, but the memory of humankind lives and will go on living as long as the human race survives. It is the duty of all of us who fought in that terrible war to make sure that it is not forgotten. Now that nuclear weapons can wipe out not only life on earth but the planet itself, the memory of the past must serve as a reminder of what wars of attrition can lead to.

Thousands of people come alive in my memory when I recall the war years. Hundreds of them I knew well, dozens of them were my friends. Every war veteran remembers people who were just as wonderful. Leafing through the pages of this book takes me back to the war years. All the faces seem familiar, even those I never met: probably because we were all soldiers fighting for the common victory.

VLADIMIR KARPOV:
Hero of the Soviet Union and writer

Operation Barbarossa

Saturday 21st June 1941 was graduation day at most schools in the Soviet Union. All over the country students talked of their plans for the future and promised to keep in touch with one another.

The morning newspapers of 22nd June carried the usual reports of industrial production and agricultural developments in different parts of the country. There was alarming news of the war Japan was waging in China, as well as accounts of fighting in North Africa and in the Middle East.

But people in the western regions had been woken at 4 am by the sound of falling bombs and collapsing buildings. The Soviet Union had been invaded by a German army of three million men, along a 4,000-mile front. Only at 5.30 that same morning did the German ambassador, Count von Schulenburg, hand over his government's memorandum with the declaration of war. By that time the Luftwaffe had already struck the airfields and troop concentrations of the Red Army, wiping out several hundred planes and tanks and other equipment before they could be deployed for action. Communications were disrupted, both between Soviet army units and between the units and the General Headquarters of the Armed Forces. In the first few days of the war, therefore, the Red Army's resistance to the German war machine was only sporadic. The reason for this lay in the recent history of Soviet–German relations.

Although there had been a German/Soviet non-aggression pact since August 1939, it was becoming increasingly clear to everyone that war with Germany was inevitable. However, the Soviet armed forces were not yet ready to take on Germany, so Josef Stalin, the Russian leader, had to keep playing for time. Even at the very last moment, when he had been warned that a German attack was likely on 21st or 22nd June, he ordered border troops not to be drawn into opening fire. It has been suggested that he thought Hitler was bluffing. Stalin was convinced that Hitler would try to provoke skirmishes which could then be used as an excuse for an invasion of Russia. Stalin was so determined not to give Hitler any justification for an attack that he forbade massive troop build-up along the border. As a result the country was almost wholly unprepared for the invasion, and within a month the Wehrmacht was halfway to Moscow.

The leadership was faced with massive, and apparently insoluble problems. There were several major priorities – stopping the German advance, gearing the country's economy to war, mobilizing the army, evacuating everything of value for industry, farming, science and culture from the Western regions, and defending the population.

Noise detectors used to sense approaching planes. They were first used during World War I and were fairly efficient, although they gave way to more sophisticated equipment.

Hitler described the invasion, which he code-named Operation Barbarossa, as the largest military operation in history. He was probably right. The invading force consisted of three Army Groups. Army Group Centre, heading for Moscow, consisted of 50 divisions, fifteen of them armoured, with 1,630 planes for air support. Army Group North – 29 divisions, including 6 armoured divisions and 760 combat planes – was advancing on the Baltic republics, aiming to take Leningrad and the Soviet naval stronghold of Kronstadt. Army Group South – 57 divisions, 9 armoured, with 1,650 planes – was advancing towards Kiev and Odessa.

In 1941 the German Wehrmacht had 8.5 million men, 5,639 tanks and assault guns, over 10,000 planes and more than 61,000 guns and mortars. The Navy had at its command 217 fighting ships, including 161 submarines. The German troops' morale was at its peak. In two years they had conquered Poland, Norway, Denmark, Holland, Belgium, France, Yugoslavia and Greece, encountering very little resistance on the way. They now believed themselves to be invincible.

The Soviet Armed Forces comprised 5.3 million men, 1,860 of a new type of tank (in addition to the 17,000 obsolescent tanks), over 2,700 new planes, 67,000 guns and mortars and a considerable amount of outdated equipment. The Soviet Navy consisted of 276 warships,

The invasion of Russia: Operation Barbarossa.

20

A mother says goodbye to her son as he leaves for the front.

including 212 submarines. The morale of the Red Army had been seriously undermined by the purge of the officer corps in 1937–38, and most of the population had suffered to a greater or lesser extent during the upheavals of the civil war and of the 1920s and 1930s.

Consequently, Hitler was convinced that the conquest of the Soviet Union would prove no problem for his battle-hardened troops: the war would be over in six weeks, he thought. At first, his confidence seemed to be justified. Within a fortnight of the invasion half a million Russians had been killed. Of the 170 Red Army divisions that had been stationed near the western frontier on 22nd June, 28 had ceased to exist, and 70 had been halved in numbers and equipment. By September the enemy troops had captured Lithuania, Latvia, Estonia, Belorussia, Moldavia, part of Greater Russia and the Ukraine. Despite heavy casualties – over 530,000 men by the beginning of October – they kept driving eastwards.

The German generals wanted to concentrate on taking Moscow. Hitler, however, insisted that the main objectives were the capture of Leningrad and of the Caucasus in the south. But in September he changed his mind, and launched Operation Typhoon, an all-out attack on Moscow with over half a million troops. He spelt out his intention in a Directive to the Eastern Front: 'We finally have the prerequisites for the last shattering blow which is to lead to the annihilation of the enemy before the onset of winter.'

The Germans began bombing Moscow at the end of July. As in London, the Metro system was used to provide shelter during air-raids. All the trains were stopped, and mothers and babies were allowed to sleep in the carriages. Platforms and passages were also reserved for families – unaccompanied adults usually had to sleep on the rails. After the first few weeks a library organization was started in these shelters; people could borrow books or magazines and read them on special benches during attacks.

At the outbreak of war private radio sets had been commandeered, but most apartment houses were equipped with loudspeakers over which wireless programmes and air-raid warnings were broadcast. There were sirens on the streets, but most people made for shelter when they heard the soothing voice on the radio say quietly: 'Trevoga! Citizens, take cover!'

Fire-watching was organized in blocks of flats by the House Committees. These committees had existed before the war, to organize repairs and maintenance, to administer services, to collect rents and to adjudicate in disputes between tenants. Now, they drew up rotas of tenants for firewatching and extinguishing incendiary bombs. Air-raid protection was the responsibility of the City and district Soviets. By the autumn, in the streets of Moscow all shop-fronts had been boarded over and sandbagged, to prevent danger from broken glass. But, despite the fact that they were used to living with the threat of air-raids, Muscovites did not seriously expect the enemy to reach the capital. Such an eventuality was unthinkable.

The Soviet troops made desperate stands at each defensive line before their capital, but the Germans were still advancing ten miles a day along a 400-mile front. They captured the town of Orel, 200 miles south-west of Moscow, so quickly that the trams were still running when the German tanks rolled in. Local people going off to work cheered what they thought was the arrival of the Red Army.

In the first week of October the rains came, and the roads turned to mud. The German tanks and armoured vehicles had great difficulty in moving, but they kept going, and were still covering, on average, four miles a day. The authorities evacuated government bodies, the diplomatic corps and major armaments factories from Moscow to Kuibyshev, 200 miles to the south-east. On 15th, 16th and 17th October the Muscovites suddenly seemed to lose their nerve. There was panic in the city as the enemy reached Khimki, halfway beween the airport and the Kremlin. But, just as suddenly, Moscow's resistance stiffened. At this point Stalin appointed Army General (later Marshal) Georgi Zhukov, who had organized the defence of Leningrad, to take command of the Red Army in the Moscow area. On 19th October Moscow was declared to be under siege, and the civilian population was organized to build anti-tank defences around the city.

In the middle of November the temperature dropped sharply, and the ground froze. The Germans were delighted – at last the Panzers could move again. But they soon realized just how ill-equipped they were for the Russian winter. The soldiers had not been issued with cold-weather clothing, since it was believed that none would be necessary: after all, Hitler insisted that the Wehrmacht would be in Moscow before the cold weather set in.

During the next few days the barometer continued to drop. At 20° below freezing, German vehicles and artillery could no longer function. By the end of November the Russian climate was killing more Germans than the artillery of the Red Army.

On Friday 5th December, at 3 am, the first Soviet counter-attack opened, with the 31st Army attacking to the south of Moscow. Just before midday the 29th Army attacked to the north. This offensive began with the knowledge that the Japanese were not intending to attack from the east. Reports from Richard Sorge, Stalin's master spy in Tokyo, provided this valuable information. Consequently, the fresh, well-equipped Siberian units could be brought in to help repel the Germans from the suburbs of Moscow.

The Red Army maintained its attack into the New Year, and would probably have managed to capture most of the German Army Group Centre had not Hitler finally permitted it to retreat, on 15th January 1942. The Nazis had already been drawing back for some time in a ragged fashion. The official command made it possible to coordinate the retreat to Rzhev, 90 miles west of Moscow. There they managed to hold their ground, until the thaw once again immobilized both armies.

The Germans continued to occupy the western territories, planning huge initiatives for the early summer. But the myth of their invincibility had been broken. The Blitzkrieg would never be the same again. The Russian people also felt hopeful because on 7th December, two days after the counter-attack, the Japanese had bombed Pearl Harbor, and America entered the war.

Moscow, noon, Sunday 22nd June 1941. Public address systems on every street corner broadcast the announcement by Stalin's Foreign Commissar, Vyacheslav Molotov, of the German invasion. The invasion was, according to the Germans, in response to a Soviet breach of the Nazi–Soviet Pact of 23rd August 1939. Molotov described the German action as 'an unparalleled act of perfidy in the history of civilized nations'. Recalling how the Russian people had risen to crush Napoleon's invasion in 1812, he concluded by calling upon Russian citizens to rally closely round 'the glorious Bolshevik Party, around the Soviet Government and our great leader Comrade Stalin. Our cause is good. The enemy will be smashed. Victory will be ours.'

Wives and children accompany troops on their way to the front.

23rd June 1941: volunteers enlisting for the army. About 2 million people volunteered during 1941 and 1942. Some units were composed entirely of volunteers at the beginning of the war, but by 1943 this situation had changed because the losses of highly-trained professional and technical experts in these units were very high.

The Red Army parading with the 14.5mm PTRS 1941 anti-tank rifle. Because of their liking for fighting at close quarters, Russian troops were equipped with anti-tank rifles long after their Western Allies and Axis enemies had discarded them as obsolete. In fact, four types of anti-tank rifle were used by the Red Army.

Our unit was stationed in the Ukraine, at Proskurovo, a town that was a short distance from the border. On 21st June we returned late from exercise and were relieved to hear the order to retire after supper. Nothing foretold of misfortune. I clearly recall that the star-strewn black sky looked fathomless as I walked to the barracks. At about 4 am the bombs came down on the town and in another half-hour we were engaged in furious combat with a German airborne landing on the outskirts of our town. None of us knew at the time, nor could we know, that 1,418 days and nights would have to pass before we wreaked vengeance on the fascist sadists for the havoc they caused our peaceful nation, for the tears of our mothers and children.

In his speech following the German invasion in 1941, Stalin said: 'Whenever units of the Red Army are forced to retreat . . . the collective farmers must drive away all their livestock, hand their grain reserves to the State organs for evacuation to the rear . . . all valuable property, whether grain, fuel or non-ferrous metals, which cannot be evacuated, must be destroyed.' Here, animals are seen being evacuated to the east. It is said that some cows were forced to walk up to 160 kilometres (100 miles) without being milked, fed or given water.

A familiar sight in a devastated village. All that remains of the wooden house is the old iron stove. In the ruins of thousands of homes families crouched around the stove, and while healthy adults slept on the ground, young children, old people and cats would sleep on top of the stove, desperate for warmth.

Facing page: *The Ukraine, July 1941. A village in flames in the wake of Field Marshal von Rundstedt's advance towards the oilfields of the Caucasus. After the war it was claimed that the Germans destroyed 6 million houses, leaving 25 million people homeless.*

A wounded soldier being helped from the battlefield, summer 1941. In that year the Russian army had very few automatics; most soldiers were equipped with rifles.

A Soviet soldier bringing in a wounded comrade from the battlefield, summer 1941.

General (later Marshal) Ivan Koniev at the Moscow front, autumn 1941, with a group of Soviet writers, who worked as war correspondents for Red Star *and* Pravda. *The group includes Alexander Fadeyev, a novelist, Alexei Surkov, known as the 'soldiers' poet', and, the most famous, Mikhail Sholokov, author of* Quiet Flows the Don. *As a result of their contributions, the literary quality of war reporting was extremely high in the Soviet Press.*

The river Viliya in Lithuania is where I received my baptism of fire, on the sixth day of the war. With immense difficulty we built a pontoon bridge across the river and in the morning, our combat and logistics units and our medical teams crossed to the other side. They were followed by an endless stream of refugees herding livestock. The crossing was taking a long time and soon there were crowds of people and vehicles on the river bank. That was when the German bombers came. What followed will never be erased from my memory. The people on the road ran for cover to the forest, jumped into the river, to the side of the road, but death overtook them everywhere. A bomb tore into the teeming mass and I was pinned to the ground by something hot and sticky. When I came round I realized that I was lying under the mutilated pieces of what had once been someone's body. The earth was burning, boxes with cartridges and shells were blowing up and the bridge we had put up with such difficulty was blasted. It took us an hour after the planes had gone to organize the people, to dig up those who had been buried under debris, and to give first aid to the wounded. With heavy hearts we interred the dead sappers by the river and put up a modest obelisk to them – a tree that had been stripped of its bark. All through the war we remembered this first common grave and the obelisk . . .

The night bombing of
Berlin: a Soviet view.
Berlin was raided for the
first time by the Red Air
Force on 11th–12th
August 1941, when the
Nazi capital was attacked
by Petlyakov Pc 8
bombers of the 332
Special Purposes Heavy
Bomber Regiment.

A Pc-8 bomber of the type used in the raid on Berlin.

A bomb inscribed 'A Present for Hitler'.

Children in Odessa helping to build sandbag barricades. The city was besieged by one German and 18 Rumanian divisions between 5th August and 16th October 1941. Half the population – some 350,000 inhabitants – were able to evacuate by sea. Rumanian losses were high: 110,000 according to the Russians, 70,000 according to Bucharest. Odessa, together with Moscow, Leningrad, Stalingrad and Kiev, was to rank as a 'hero city'.

Singers from the Bolshoi Theatre firewatching in August 1941. Firewatching was organized on a vast scale, and during the first air-raids many firewatchers were badly injured by incendiary bombs – sometimes because they would pick up the bombs with their bare hands. The penalties for neglecting your duty were severe. In one case, three men held responsible for the destruction of a warehouse worth 3 million roubles were shot.

The Nazis broke into Sokal, a town in the Western Ukraine, after a savage fight . . . A tank made straight for the ruins of what had been the border command post where, in the basement, women and children had taken cover.

At that moment a man in flaming clothes dashed towards the armoured monster. Tearing off his burning coat he threw it on the grille of the engine hatch and then flung himself like a blazing torch under the tank. An explosion followed. The fascists turned back . . .

This occurred on the first day of the war, 22nd June, at about 9 am.

A Red Army soldier sighting a 12.7mm DShK 1938 machine-gun, the standard Soviet heavy machine-gun for the duration of the war.

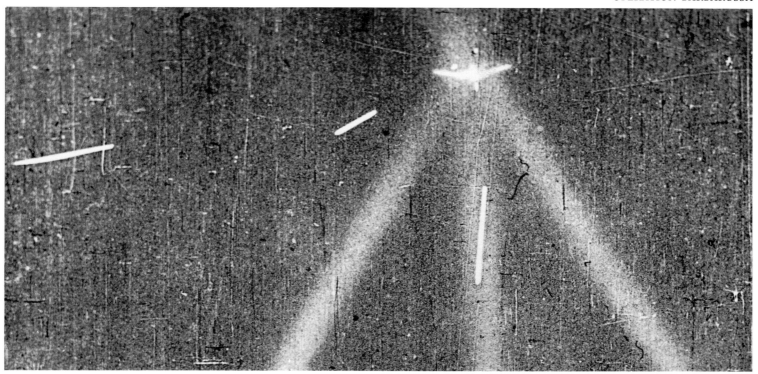

A German plane caught in a searchlight; Soviet tracer shells bursting around their target.

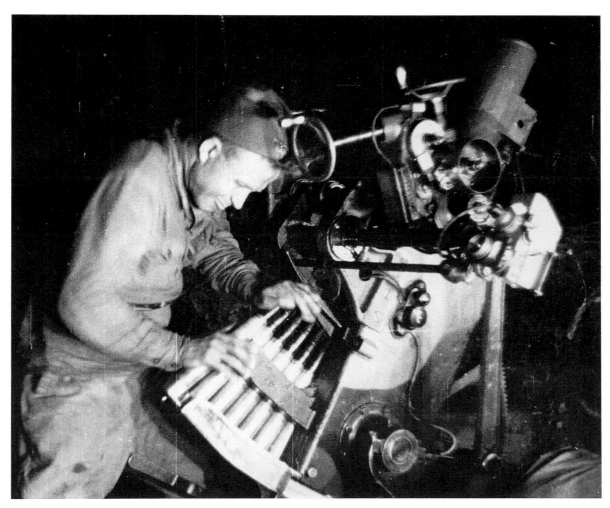

Inserting shells into the 37mm anti-aircraft gun model 1939. Its rate of fire was 80 rounds per minute; each shell weighed 0.785kg (1.73 lb).

The battle for Sebastopol lasted 250 days, from 30th October 1941 to 4th July 1942, when the city finally fell to the Germans. Here the Soviet battleship Parishskaya Kommuna (Paris Commune), formerly the Sebastopol, fires its main armament at German positions.

The Russians were outnumbered two to one at the battle of Sebastopol by the German and Rumanian invaders. Here, a nurse rolls a cigarette for a wounded soldier, among those evacuated from Sebastopol.

The Sacred War

Arise, vast Land, in awesome might!
For mortal combat gird
Against the evil powers of night,
The fascist hordes accursed!
Let storms of indignation rage
And righteous wrath outpour!
This is a sacred war we wage,
A people's sacred war.

This was the most famous of the songs sung during World War II.
Y. A. Yemelyanov, a veteran member of the choir, recalls: 'As we took our places on the makeshift platform I wondered if we would be able to perform in such conditions. The huge waiting-room was packed and noisy. Talk, clipped orders, radio announcements . . .

Alexandrov raised his baton and with the first few notes the hall fell silent. By the time we were into the second verse everyone was standing, as though the anthem was being played. There were tears in many eyes. Ours too. On the insistence of the audience we sang it 5 times . . .'

Marines during an assault. They were known as 'the Black Death' to their German opponents, because their uniforms were black and because they were among the best fighters of all the Soviet troops.

Murmansk: '. . . and then he . . .', a Soviet airman describes an air combat. Russian flyers were nicknamed 'Stalin Hawks'.

Murmansk: only the chimneys remain of what was once a town, as a homeless family flees the Germans. The port, vital for British supplies to the Soviet Union, was mostly destroyed in a great fire blitz in June 1942.

An Anglo-Soviet soccer match at Murmansk, the northern port on the Barents Sea. No. 135 Wing, Royal Air Force, had been sent to provide air cover for convoys of arms and other equipment. They were flying Hawker Hurricanes.

About half a million civilians – women, children, and old people – dug anti-tank ditches outside Moscow. Before they could begin digging, fires were lit to thaw the ground. The Germans bombed and machine-gunned these civilians frequently, killing many and causing large numbers of casualties.

Barrage balloons on the streets of Moscow, 1941. Barrage balloons were used extensively in the defence of Moscow. They forced the German bombers to fly higher, which made their bombing less accurate.

Moscow, October 1941. A barrage balloon in front of the Bolshoi Theatre.

Sandbag barricades on Smolensk Street, Moscow. As the Germans of Heeresgruppe Mitte *(Army Group Centre) advanced on the capital, these emergency measures were put into operation so that the Muscovites were prepared should they reach the heart of the city.*

After intense fighting we were forced to leave Daugavpils. The city was an inferno of burning houses and bursting shells. Suddenly, in the very thick of the street fighting, a woman with an infant in her arms appeared from nowhere. She was terrified out of her wits and kept screaming for someone to save her baby. To the left, a company was advancing. The lieutenant, who looked as though he was just a teenager, noticed the woman and rushed to her aid without a second thought. We opened fire to cover him. He took the child from the woman and grabbing her by the wrist ran to a nearby apartment house. He was out in a matter of three minutes and ran to catch up with his company. At that very moment a shell struck in front of us. I happened to be the closest to the lieutenant and rushed to help him. One of his legs had been torn off above the knee. I took off my belt and pulled it tight above the wound to staunch the blood.

I've been through the war and I've seen many badly wounded people. But never before or after did I see such bravery. The lieutenant smiled and said in farewell: 'This is not important. What counts is that I rescued that woman and her baby.' I will never forgive myself for not remembering the name of that boy . . .

Children in a slit trench during an air-raid over Moscow, late summer 1941.

Josef Stalin speaking from the rostrum during the traditional celebrations to mark the anniversary of the October Revolution in 1917, on 7th November 1941. By this time the Germans had reached the outskirts of the city. The decision to go ahead with the parade, and the presence of Stalin, boosted the morale of the Muscovites, which had been badly affected by scenes of panic on 16th October.

In his speech, Stalin drew comparisons with the first anniversary in 1918, when the situation was much worse, but the power of Lenin's great spirit inspired the people to rise against the enemy; he recalled great Russian heroes of the past, concluding: 'The war you are waging is a war of liberation, a just war. May you be inspired in this war by the heroic figures of our great ancestors Alexander Nevsky, Dmitri Donskoi, Minin and Pozharsky, Alexander Suvorov, Mikhail Kutuzov! May you be blest by great Lenin's victorious banner! Death to the German invaders! Long live our glorious country, its freedom and independence! Under the banner of Lenin – onward to victory!'

After the parade, tanks drive down Gorky Street, heading for the front. As soon as the celebrations were over, all the military personnel and equipment involved returned directly to the front. It was said that the Germans had been planning their own Red Square celebrations for after the capture of the city and had already printed invitations to it! Hitler had hoped that the war with Russia would be over by November. In fact, the Germans advanced no further than Istra, fifteen miles west of Moscow.

Bullseye! A direct hit on a German tank.

Facing page: *Families sleeping in the Mayakovsky metro station. All the deep metro stations in Moscow were used as air-raid shelters. The Moscow metro was seen as one of the greatest achievements of the pre-war Soviet régime when it opened in 1935.*

Loading a Field Howitzer, model 1910/30. This First World War piece had a range of 8,940 metres (9,780 yds) and its shells weighed 21.76 kilograms (47.98 lb). This type of gun was useful for bombarding a target several miles away that was not visible. It lobbed its powerful shells in a high arc.

Facing page: *December 1941. Ammunition being taken to the front by horse-drawn sledge, passing in front of the Kremlin.*

December 1941. At a newspaper kiosk civilians read about the progress of the battle of Moscow. The man in the foreground was almost certainly a worker in a vital industry, such as munitions, because, by that time, most workers in the less essential industries had been evacuated to the east. By 7th November 1941, half the population had left the capital. Stalin, however, remained in Moscow throughout the battle.

The defence of Moscow. Winter clothing, such as these sheepskin coats, was a crucial factor in the battle for Moscow. Hitler had always maintained that his troops would not need warm clothing. The war in Russia would be over, he insisted, before the cold set in. Not all the Soviet troops had coats as warm as these, but for those who did, they were ideal. They were especially welcome when troops had to stand for hours on end in trenches, waist high in snow, in sub-zero temperatures. The troops are equipped with 14.5mm anti-tank rifles PTRS 1941 and the 7.62mm 1910 Russian Maxim machine-gun, which bore a strong resemblance to the British Vickers gun.

A 1910 Maxim 7.62mm machine-gun in action. The Maxim was belt-fed, water-cooled and operated on the recoil principle. It was issued with two different types of mounting – the popular 'Sokolov' (named after its designer) consisted of a wheeled carriage and a U-shaped trail (shown here); and the Universal mounting, a proper tripod. Both mounts could be fitted with a steel shield to protect the gunner. It had two sights – a folding bar rear sight, and a barleycorn foresight, set to the left to avoid the water inlets. A bracket for an optical sight was sometimes fixed to the left side of the breech.

A private soldier entertains his friends with a display of the traditional Russian men's dancing, in the tiring and difficult squatting position.

Facing page: *A Soviet sentry in Red Square, by Lenin's tomb, in November 1941. The depth of snow demonstrates the unusual severity of the winter that year.*

I remember we were trying to take a little hill that was to give us control over a locality . . . Three times we attacked and each time we were thrown back. The enemy opened up drumfire. I was sent on a scouting mission. That was when I witnessed the following incident. A Soviet soldier was walking erect toward the hill. He was wounded, alone, without weapons. The Germans watched him closely. When he was about 30 metres from them, the soldier took out a harmonica and started playing a lovely Russian melody on it. The Nazis started to clamber out of cover and soon they had practically surrounded the man. The last thing I saw was a grenade explosion and the Germans being thrown in different directions. The soldier had blown himself up together with the enemy.

The Russian counter-offensive in the Moscow area began on 5th–6th December, along a 560-mile front. Here, Russian soldiers storm an occupied village on the city's western outskirts.

Russian troops counter-attack near Moscow, 5th–6th December 1941. Fresh Siberian troops, well equipped to withstand the cold weather, and accustomed to much worse, were brought to Moscow to join this offensive. Camouflage suits, as in the picture, were of great importance for fighting in the snow. Germans, without such suits, were known to improvise by using looted tablecloths or sheets. In this photograph the soldiers carry sub-machine-guns, which were very rare in the Soviet army in those days.

A road near Moscow after the German retreat. During the battle for Moscow temperatures dropped to −40° Centigrade. The Russians understood such conditions – the Germans had never known anything like it. Automatic weapons, frozen, would only fire once. But as the Germans retreated, abandoning their useless weapons, they would see Soviet troops pick them up, lubricate them with the correct oil for such conditions and immediately use them.

After a long battle for Davydovo, a village in the Moscow region, our company was given permission to clean up. It was almost morning and we started looking for a well. We knocked on the very first door. An old man who'd been frightened by the night battle pointed to the other end of the village: 'It ought to be there', he said, 'if the Nazis didn't blow it up before retreating.' The well was there, undamaged. But when we glanced inside our blood ran cold. The well was full of the corpses of children, from tiny infants to some about five years old.

'Tatchianka', Maxim machine-guns mounted on horse-drawn carts. These carts with guns were very effective during the Civil War in Russia. By 1941 they were obviously completely outdated, but they were still used when necessary.

Kalinin, named after one of the heroes of the Revolution, was liberated during the December counter-offensive. Here, on 16th December, guns are pulled through the streets of the city by horses.

Surveying the damage at Yasnaya Polyana, Leo Tolstoy's house. The Germans had occupied the building until they were thrown out in December 1941. They had looted and badly damaged the house and buried their dead around Tolstoy's solitary grave. The house is now a museum.

The War Effort

In the middle of July 1941, barely three weeks after the German invasion, a British correspondent in Moscow attended a performance of a play entitled *In the Ukrainian Steppes*, in which one of the characters made this announcement: 'There is nothing more maddening than being interrupted just as you are completing the roof of your hut: if only we had five more years! But if war comes then we shall fight with a fierceness and anger the like of which the world has never seen.' This brought the house down. The correspondent felt that this 'was an excellent summing up of the Russians' attitude to the war'. Overnight every aspect of life had to be geared to the war effort, and for the next four years the slogan 'Everything for the front. Everything for Victory!' was to be seen throughout the Soviet Union.

Early in July 1941 the Council for Evacuation was formed, to organize the removal of industrial plants and national treasures to areas far away from the fighting. The Council's decisions were endorsed by the government, and were to be obligatory for all.

The evacuation began within days of the invasion. On 2nd July it was decided that the armoured-plate mill at Mariupol, in the Southern Ukraine, should be moved to Magnitogorsk, although Mariupol was still hundreds of miles from the front line. Dozens of other factories in the Russian Federation, the Ukraine, Belorussia, the Baltic Republics and Moldavia were evacuated at this time, usually under enemy fire. On 3rd July the State Defence Committee, after approving the plans for weapons production for the next few months, decided to transfer 26 armaments plants from Moscow, Leningrad and Tula to the east, and during the same week it was decided to evacuate some of the equipment and staff from the diesel department of the Kirovsky Tractor Plant in Leningrad and the Tractor Plant in Kharkov.

Other industries were converted for wartime purposes. The Gorki Automobile Plant concentrated on the production of tank engines, and a vast Volga-Urals combine for mass-producing tanks was established. Similar procedures were adopted in the aircraft industry. One factory, evacuated on 9th August, arrived in the Urals on 6th September and was in full production again by 24th September. From Kiev alone 197 major industrial plants were evacuated in just two months. Altogether, between July and November 1941, 1,523 industrial enterprises, including 1,360 large armaments plants, were moved to the east; 226 were sent to the Volga area, 667 to the Urals, 244 to Western Siberia, 78 to Eastern Siberia and 308 to Kazakhstan and Central Asia.

Some of the evacuated plants were sent to affiliated factories, enabling them to increase their production capacity substantially. As often as not, the evacuated equipment was assembled out in the open in the worst possible weather conditions during autumn and winter. However, several plants began to function again six weeks or so after they had arrived at their destination.

Ivan Kozhedub, the most successful Soviet fighter pilot of the war, shot down 60 enemy planes without ever losing his own aircraft. He began the war as a sergeant, because he had already undergone a crash course in flying. He was made a Hero of the Soviet Union three times, and is now Marshal of the Air Force. The plane in the photograph was donated by the collective farmer Koniev.

In Tashkent, the capital of Uzbekistan, for example, 100,000 square metres of industrial space was constructed within a matter of weeks for the 23 factories that arrived from the west. The Chkalov aircraft-building plant, evacuated from Moscow, produced its first plane 40 days after it arrived. Extraordinary difficulties were overcome. A munitions factory that arrived from Rostov-on-Don left its foundry behind in the confusion of evacuation. The foundry had taken two years to build, but a replacement was constructed in 28 days.

At the same time, Tashkent, with its pre-war population of 700,000 people, was adjusting to the arrival of 200,000 evacuees, including 40,000 children. Uzbekistan as a whole was accommodating 2,000,000 people on top of its own population of 6,200,000 people. The first problem for the local authorities was housing. At first the new arrivals were squeezed into spare rooms or corners of rooms in existing buildings. But soon it became necessary to construct single-storey adobe shelters for the newcomers.

The second difficulty was feeding the evacuees. Every factory, as soon as it was relocated, was given land which the workers cultivated after they had finished working on the shop-floor. Moscow sent seeds, and the Uzbekistan authorities lent horses for ploughing the land. They also arranged for the armaments factories to produce a limited amount of agricultural machinery. Individual families also grew as many vegetables as they could.

The first wave of evacuation hit Uzbekistan between July 1941 and February 1942. A lull followed, but then the German offensive in the North Caucasus sent a second wave of refugees eastwards from July to December 1942.

Despite the extraordinary difficulties it faced, the achievements of Soviet industry during the war were remarkable. Up until 1943 it was still recovering from the evacuation, but thereafter tank production was phenomenal. In that year 16,000 heavy and medium tanks were produced, 4,000 mobile guns and 3,500 light tanks. This total was eight and a half times more than in 1940

The actors of the Moscow Mali Theatre Company raised 1½ million roubles to build the 'Mali Theatre Squadron' of military aircraft, and presented the planes to the pilots. Here, Turchaninova, Yablochkina, Rizhova and Poliakov, members of the theatre company, watch the planes doing aerobatics at an airfield near Moscow.

and nearly four times more than in 1941. The average monthly output of tanks rose from 2,100 at the end of 1942 to 2,900 in 1943. In 1943 35,000 planes were produced, 37% more than in 1942. At the height of the battle of Kursk, in the summer of 1943, more than 1,000 *stormoviks* (the Il-2 plane) were being produced every month.

According to Stalin, speaking in 1946, between 1942 and 1945 the Soviet Union produced about 100,000 tanks, 120,000 aeroplanes, 360,000 guns, over 1,200,000 machine guns, 6,000,000 tommy guns, 9,000,000 rifles, 300,000 mortars, some 700,000,000 shells and some 20 billion cartridges. From the end of 1941, the USA and Great Britain sent weapons, planes and tanks to help the war effort. This equipment amounted to 4% of the Soviet total.

Armaments production was not restricted to factories far behind the lines. In Sebastopol, besieged by German and Rumanian forces, 400 mine-throwers, 20,000 hand-grenades and 32,000 anti-personnel mines were produced during November and December 1941. Thousands of other items such as tanks, guns and rifles were repaired by the besieged garrison and the city's inhabitants.

On 26th June 1941 a law on working hours in wartime came into effect, giving managers on the farms and in the factories the right to impose compulsory overtime work every day. Holidays were suspended for the duration of the war: workers would receive extra pay instead. All able-bodied men were needed at the front: during the first eight days of the war alone 5,300,000 were called up, and thousands more volunteered for the armed services. In the workshops and in the fields they had to be replaced by women and adolescents who had quickly been taught the basic skills. Still the situation grew worse as the months went by. On 26th December 1941 the Supreme Soviet passed a law under which absence without leave, in any industry involved in the war effort, was viewed as desertion.

By 1942 about 70 million people had been trapped on enemy-occupied territory. The country was faced with a terrible manpower shortage. The only solution to this was longer working hours. In many factories the normal working week, for those over eighteen years of age, was 66 hours. Employees were paid on a time-and-a-half basis for overtime, and were also awarded bonuses if they exceeded their quotas. As a result, although the basic minimum wage at this time was between 200 and 400 roubles a month, it was not unusual for workers to be taking home 1,000 roubles.

From 1st November 1941 food rationing was introduced throughout the country. But the availability of food varied widely from place to place. In some areas close to the front people were unable to get hold of even the minimum amount of food to which the ration entitled them. On the other hand, towns that were surrounded by collective farms, out of reach of the invaders, suffered no serious food shortages.

Where food was available it was possible to buy more than the ration, but at higher prices. For example, butter on the ration cost between 26 and 28 roubles a kilo in 1941. In the more expensive, but perfectly legal, shops that sold unrationed butter, it cost 50 roubles per kilo. Similarly, sugar was 5.50 roubles a kilo normally, but anyone who wanted more than their ration book entitled them to had to pay 15 roubles for the same amount. Rationed bread cost between 1.70 and 3.50, according to the type of loaf. Unrationed, it cost exactly twice as much.

This system did not entirely eradicate black marketeering, but it restricted it. The Government, in effect, cornered the market in surplus food. The fact that, with appalling exceptions, the population did not have to endure serious food shortages, was due to efficient planning and a successful campaign to cultivate new agricultural land. The occupation of the western territories, especially the Ukraine, traditionally the bread basket of the Russian empire, was a serious blow to the country's food supplies. In 1942 the country's farms produced a third as much grain as in 1940, two thirds of the meat and slightly less than half the milk and dairy produce. People were encouraged to grow food wherever they could, to make up for this loss, and allotments were given to groups of office and industrial workers.

Clothing was rationed according to a system of coupons, similar to the method employed in Britain at the time. A heavy industrial worker would be given 100 units every three months, a clerical worker 80 units. A pair of men's trousers would take 25 of these units, a shirt 20, a pair of underpants 12, a pair of socks 2 and a pair of shoes 20. Household linen was included in the same coupon system: a blanket took 30 units, a pillowcase 12. Soap was included in the Clothing Coupon Book. Each person was entitled to one bar of toilet soap and one of washing soap each week. Clothing, like food, could occasionally be bought without coupons at more expensive shops.

It is clear from these figures that so long as the supplies were available (which was often not the case) they were adequate to provide the civilian population with food and clothing.

Nevertheless, the erratic wartime situation meant that the Russian housewife, who was not unused to queuing in peacetime, would now have to spend even longer waiting in line to make essential purchases, or visiting one shop after another to find what she needed. This was no joke for women who were working overtime every day in the factories.

Although Soviet industry was largely staffed by women at this time, thousands of women also volunteered to serve in the armed services. They joined the Red Army or the Red Air Force, which had three regiments – two bomber and one fighter – consisting entirely of women. By the end of 1941, 8% of those in the Red Army were women, although this figure includes front-line medical personnel. The Red Cross and Red Crescent organizations trained 400,000 women, who went to the front as doctors, nurses, orderlies and stretcher-bearers. Throughout the country women were also prominent in civil defence and firewatching operations.

The war effort even involved children. Encouraged by the local Komsomol organizations, they visited wounded soldiers in hospitals or organized salvage collections. At first, schoolboys found it exciting to gather fragments of anti-aircraft shells, still warm, to be re-used by the armaments industry. Children stayed after hours in their school workshops making tin mugs, gun parts and packing cases for the armaments factories. Others helped to sew clothing for the Red Army, and hospital bed linen and bandages. A teacher commented at the time: 'Before the war, we brought up children rather differently, paying much attention to their spiritual development. But this cruel war forces us to mobilize all the country's resources – even the immature power and abilities of our children.'

Children were also involved in the drive to increase food production. A hundred children from the Moscow Pioneers' Club organized themselves into gardening brigades, elected their own board of management and were given their own plot of land on which to plant vegetables. Young boys and girls volunteered to help with the Victory Fund. Children in Siberia, for example, many of whom were evacuees, gave their pocket money to the war effort. Kopeck by kopeck they raised 179,000 roubles, enough to buy a tank, which the children christened 'Baby'. Despite the dangers, the upheaval of evacuation and the distress of losing, if only temporarily, their fathers, the war had its advantages. Many found it easier to escape parental supervision, with their mothers, and all other adults, working long hours. It was possible to indulge in pursuits that would never normally have been allowed. During the winter, snow and ice were not cleared from the streets as regularly as in peacetime, so the roads became very icy. Enterprising boys discovered that there was a lot of fun to be had by clinging on to the back of a bus or tram, wearing skates, and allowing oneself to be pulled along the icy roads.

The country's intelligentsia also did its bit for the war effort. The writer Ovady Savich, who had always claimed that 'bread rolls grow on trees', was persuaded by the Writers' Union to follow Tolstoy's example and wield a spade. At the beginning of the war about 900 writers, including some of the most famous, such as Ehrenburg and Simonov, became war correspondents. Ehrenburg later recalled writing three articles a day, reading and translating German documents, intercepting German radio messages, editing translations and writing captions to photographs taken at the front. Hundreds of scientists and writers rushed to enlist in the army during the first few days of the war, and later had to be pulled out of the trenches as it became clear to the authorities that they could be of more use elsewhere.

There is no doubt that the tremendous efforts of the ordinary people in their day-to-day lives contributed greatly to the Soviet Union's eventual victory.

Actors on their way to the front to entertain troops. Popular artistes included Lubova Orlova, a Soviet Gracie Fields, and Alexander Vertinsky, who after 20 years in exile returned to the Soviet Union, and whose escapist songs became wildly popular in 1944.

Winter 1941/2. KVI tanks, named after Kliementi Voroshilov, People's Commissar for Defence, donated by a collective farm in the Moscow region.

It was the last day of the first spring month of 1943. I remember, because that was the day I received notification that my husband had been killed in action. I cried all night, remembering every single day of the war – the fear and horror of seeing enemy planes bombing our village in November 1942, the endless days in the fields from sunrise to sundown with no rest at all, and the nagging fear for the four little children I had been left with. But while I cried, my hands kept knitting the woollen socks – I had already made umpteen pairs and sent them to our soldiers. At dawn I snuffed out the candle and went outside. The sun was rising from behind the mountains. I realized at that time that sorrow was familiar to many homes, that we had to live for our children and for other people, that we had to work so that our country and our people could avenge our fathers, husbands and brothers who had given their lives fighting the accursed enemy. Early in the morning I gave the children their breakfast and covering my head with a black shawl I went out to the field. The villagers didn't see me cry. It was a routine workday . . .

During the war civilians knitted millions of scarves and pairs of socks. Most of these were collected by Party or factory organizations, and were sent to the soldiers. Occasionally, a delegation from some large organization would go to the front to hand over the goods they had produced.

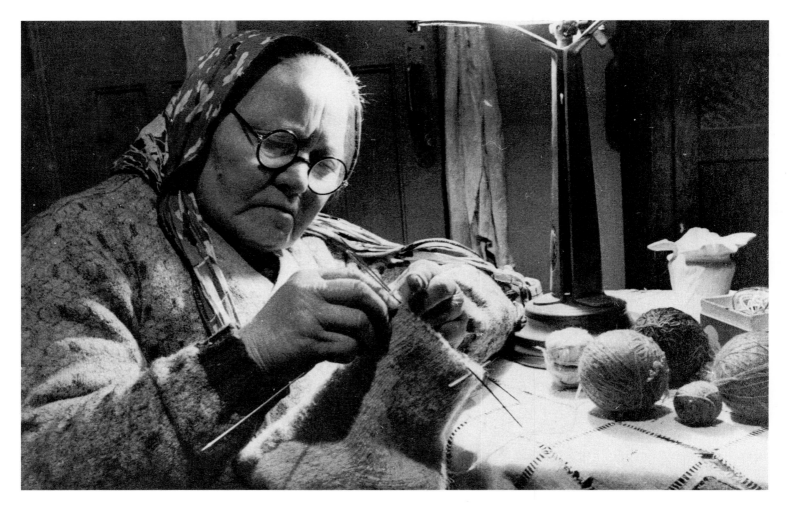

Peasants collecting money for the Defence Fund.

Silver and gold objects donated to the Defence Fund.

Packing shells in a munitions factory. As in many other countries at war, Russian women took over their husbands' jobs when the men enlisted. It helped them feel closer to their absent husbands, and they already knew about the work and the routine of the factory.

On the shop-floor of a tank factory in the Urals. The slogan on the left says – 'Produce more tanks for the Front!' The poster on the right was very popular during the war, and carries the words – 'Soldier of the Red Army, save us!'

An artillery factory in Siberia, which produced ZIS-3 76.2mm field guns, the standard Soviet field weapon. It had a range of 13,290 metres (14,540 yds) and fired a shell weighing 6.4 kilograms (14.11 lb). This gun was first produced in 1943. It could be moved easily on the battlefield and was useful in providing support for the army during an advance.

When the Germans were coming, our village had just about taken in the harvest . . . The men were away fighting and there was no one but the women, the old people and the young ones. The caterpillar tractors had gone to the fighting lines too. All we had was three old wheel tractors. We hitched the combine harvester on to them and mowed from sun-up till sundown. We also pitched in with scythes when we saw we weren't making good time. But we got all the wheat out and then it was time to drive the cattle eastwards.

We walked for almost three months. Autumn had set in . . . Four of our cows had calved and two women had given birth . . . We put the young on the carts and soon the calves were strong enough to walk on their own legs. The cows had to be milked and while you stopped to do this, the rest moved on . . . so you ran after them, milk bucket in one hand and a rod to hurry the cow along in the other. We tried to give most of the milk to the wounded in the hospitals we passed along the road. We ourselves made do with what we had brought from home and a bit of milk. That wasn't much and we were always hungry. But it never occurred to us to kill a calf for meat . . .

On 3rd July the People's Commissar for heavy machine-building, N. S. Kazakov, issued orders that the 'Krasnii Profintern' be evacuated to Krasnoyarsk in East Siberia.

We began dismantling the equipment next morning . . . Three persons loaded one freight car in less than an hour.

By the evening of 6th July, the first train was ready for send-off. It consisted of 34 freight cars carrying 334 people.

. . . Our mammoth works was to go up in what was at that time a hemp field . . . a wasteland with 4 barracks – the stores of a grain-purchasing agency . . .

. . . We managed to find lodgings for the people in the Kirov district of Krasnoyarsk in schools and community centres that were not functioning at that time. And the local people shared their homes with the new arrivals. Some offered a room, others a corner of a room . . .

It took 7,550 freight cars to evacuate the plant. Some were sent to Gorky, to Sverdlovsk, Nizhnii Tagil . . . the lion's share, more than 6 thousand freight cars, were sent to Krasnoyarsk.

During the first few weeks of the war thousands of factories were evacuated east of the Urals. Most, like this one, had to begin work again in the open air, with employees working all hours, regardless of the weather conditions.

Facing page: A train taking tanks from a factory in the east to the front. Absolute secrecy was maintained about the destination of these trains. Even the driver had no idea where he was going.

An armoured train of the sort used extensively during the first stages of the war, especially in the battle of Moscow and in the Ukraine. Each car, heavily protected by armour plates, was equipped with anti-tank guns and/or machine-guns. They were used to support the infantry, and occasionally engaged successfully with enemy tanks. These trains had been used a great deal in the Civil War, but by 1941 they were obsolete and were not replaced.

The inscription on the train reads 'Death to the German Invaders'.

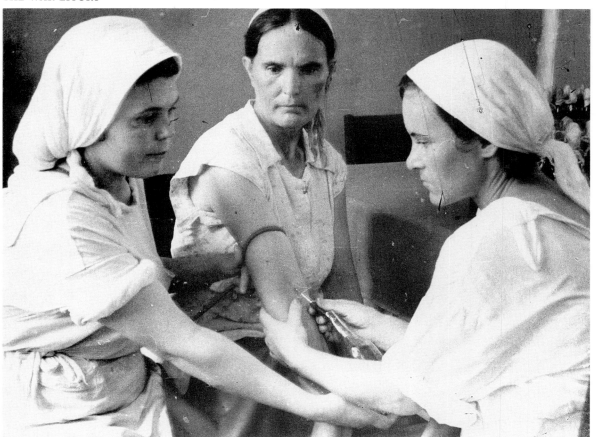

A blood donor at Ashkabad in Turkmenistan.

Exercise for wounded soldiers at a convalescent home in the Caucasus.

In the countryside after the Germans had left. As the Nazis retreated they destroyed everything they could not take with them. They slaughtered or carried off 7 million horses, 17 million cattle, 20 million pigs. They destroyed everything else – crops and buildings were flattened. It was reported that they even shipped rich black earth from the Ukraine to Germany.

His father's jacket. The child is also wearing a traditional Orenburg scarf, made from a type of wool which was very warm and very light, like cashmere.

Going to school. Few parents were able to take their children to school during the war, because the men were away fighting and the women were working in factories or on the land. As public transport was also invariably disrupted, most children had to walk to school.

Plenty of fresh air for the children in this bombed school. Everything else, however, was in short supply for wartime schoolchildren – textbooks, pencils, stationery. Teachers, children and parents used to make exercise books out of any bits of paper they could find. There was also an acute shortage of teachers during the war.

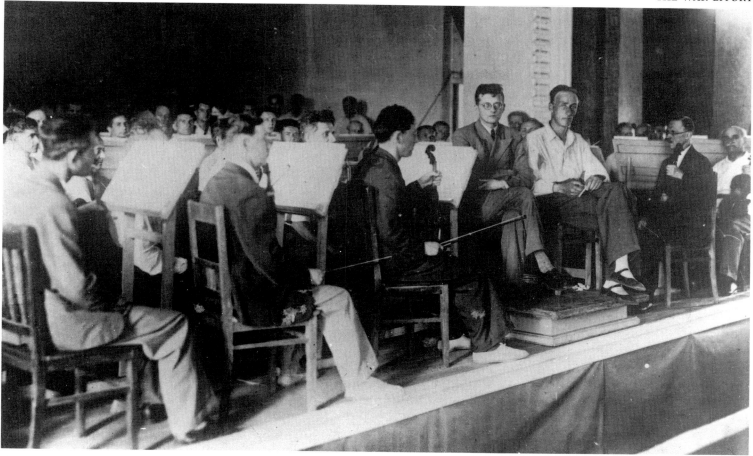

The first performance of the Leningrad Symphony by Shostakovich, in Novosibirsk, with the composer and the conductor Yevgeny Muravinsky on the platform.

In September 1941, while he was still working on the symphony, Shostakovich spoke about it on the radio:

'An hour ago I completed the score of two parts of a big symphony opus. If it turns out to be good and if I manage to complete the third and fourth parts, I will call it the Seventh Symphony. I am saying all this so that those who are listening to me now will know that the situation in our city is normal. We are all at our battle stations. . . .'

The first movement, which depicts the German invasion, was described by the British correspondent Alexander Werth as a documentary of 1941 conveying the 'naked evil in all its stupendous, arrogant inhumanity, a terrifying power overrunning Russia – there is almost nothing to equal it.'

In Turkmenistan schoolgirls pick the vital cotton crop. The best quality cotton was used in the production of gunpowder.

Summer 1942. Anti-aircraft guns (37mm model 1939) provide air cover for farmers bringing in the harvest in unoccupied territory near the front.

The water supply system was destroyed in most of the cities that the Germans occupied. Here a water truck dispenses fresh water to householders, who collect it in buckets, kettles, or whatever else they can find.

In October 1941, when the fighting was nearing Donbass, my mother, two children and I left for Uzbekistan. Our train was made up of battered old coaches and there were four adults and five children in our compartment. The very first bomber attack left us without windows and we boarded them up with sheets of plywood. Our train moved very slowly; troop and supply trains had priority.

Gradually we developed a routine that was all our own: when the train stopped, everyone went out in search of water and wood and made fires and cooked. Practically every family had brought along a couple of bricks on which to put a kettle or pot over the fire. Those who were smart had brought along an axe and they chopped whatever wood was lying along the roadside and took it with them for future use. When the engine whistled everyone grabbed whatever had been cooking on the fire and rushed for the train. All too often we left the bricks behind as they were too hot to carry. But that didn't worry us: the people in the train ahead were sure to have left similar bricks and those we left would be used by those who came after us . . . On this journey which took two months, it was the old and the sick who had the hardest time . . .

Women in the liberated territory sowing seeds by the oldest method. All their farm machinery has been destroyed, and all the farm horses have been eaten or killed during the fighting.

We were working in the field that day. I was fifteen at the time. There were only old men and young boys left in the village; practically all the work in the fields was done by our womenfolk.

We saw Naskida, the one-armed postman, coming as we sat resting under an oak. As usual, we all started rummaging in his bag. Some found letters, telegrams and newspapers . . . But Naskida was holding something in his hand and when we asked him what it was, he said abruptly that those papers were none of our business. At the same time he gave Daro a long, attentive look.

Daro was the mother of four sons, three of whom had already been killed in the war. And now there were no letters from Vakhtang, the youngest. Daro sat there crying as she usually did when she saw the postman in those days. Naskida apparently could take no more. He got up and in his eyes there was a certain something besides compassion and understanding . . .

Today, 40 years later, I know what it was . . . At his funeral recently we learned that hidden away in his home were dozens of letters notifying local families that their men had been killed in action. Daro's son, Vakhtang, was among them. For years Naskida had been carrying about the sad tidings buried deep in his heart, so that many a mother could go on waiting and hoping.

Ploughing without horses.

Two Russian peasants examine a Messerschmitt Me 109 BF fighter which has been shot down, as cows graze peacefully in the background. The aircraft's engine and other vital machinery have already been removed by the authorities.

This Uzbekh couple, the Shamakhmudovs, who had no children of their own, adopted twelve orphans of different nationalities. The three boys in front are wearing the scarves of the Soviet youth movement, the Young Pioneers.

Collective farmers in Uzbekistan giving away sheep to be sent to liberated Ukrainian villages.

The Dnieper Dam, built during the first Five Year Plan (1929–1933). It was seen as a symbol of economic progress and proof that socialism could work in Russia. It was deliberately destroyed by the Russians, according to the Soviet spokesman A. Lozovsky, on 28th August 1941, in order to deny it to the German invaders. Here, women begin rebuilding it. Its reopening, early in 1947, was seen as a triumph for the post-war reconstruction programme.

Many of us, workers at the Kharkov tractor plant, wanted to enlist, but the recruiting officers kept telling us to wait our turn. But waiting was hard. The news from the theatre of war kept getting darker every day. The enemy was approaching Leningrad . . . threatening Moscow . . . driving towards Kharkov. The word 'evacuation' was in the air.

The tractor plant had been growing for ten years. Now it had to be taken apart in the space of a few days and loaded on to freight-cars. Several thousand cars, making up many trains, were sent off on a long journey to the Altai . . .

Meanwhile, the tractor plant didn't stop functioning for a day. While the machine-tools were travelling east, the workers scraped together the last spare parts and equipment and assembled the very last tanks which they manned themselves.

Trains evacuating industrial plants were given the green light all along the way. Troop and supply trains going west were treated similarly. When the trains arrived, the machine-tools and equipment were unloaded in the open and the workers started assembling them without waiting for the shops to go up. Before the assembly line had stopped in Kharkov, the tractor plant was already operating in the Altai.

Metropolitan (Archbishop) Nikolai saying a Milebin – an Orthodox service of intercession or thanksgiving – after the battle of Moscow.

A woman working in a munitions factory which was rebuilt on liberated territory. She is wearing a hairnet to prevent her hair getting caught in the machinery. On official posters in Britain, women workers were advised to use the same type of hairnet as that used by their Russian sisters.

Overleaf: Russian factory women read Pravda *of 13th July 1941, which featured the news of the signing of the Anglo-Soviet Agreement of 12th July. The agreement provided for mutual aid and a promise not to make a separate peace. Sir Stafford Cripps, the British ambassador, signed on behalf of Great Britain, and Molotov, for the Soviet Union. The photographs on the front page show the two men signing.*

Civilians were always desperately keen to read the latest news from the front.

When the war started a group of girls at our factory, including myself, enlisted. We were assigned to a partisan unit formed in Moscow and given basic training in the special skills needed for guerrilla warfare and taught to use a rifle, a machine-gun and grenades.

I was wounded in a battle when the odds were heavily against us. Both legs and my hipbone were shattered. But I managed to crawl to the forest where I lay semi-conscious on the snow all night. In the morning I was found by some partisans and they made me as comfortable as possible in a dugout. When I was evacuated to Moscow both my legs had to be amputated. I was only 20 years old at the time and my life was just beginning. . . .

As soon as I was discharged from hospital I went back to my factory. It wasn't at all easy to stand a shift with my artificial limbs, but the thought that it was no easier where the fighting was kept me going.

These women came to Stalingrad to help with the reconstruction of the city. They were temporarily housed in this wrecked German transport plane, a Junkers Ju 52 trimotor.

The rebuilding of the city began during the summer of 1943. It would have been cheaper and easier to build a new city elsewhere, but civic pride demanded that Stalingrad should be rebuilt on its old site.

Women building new houses after the battle of Stalingrad.

Facing page: Women carrying out reconstruction work in the devastated liberated areas.

The Siege of Leningrad

Soon after invading the Soviet Union, Hitler focused his attack on Leningrad, with the intention of razing it to the ground. He saw the city of Lenin, always described as the 'cradle of the Great October Revolution', as a symbol of communism. He was determined to destroy it forever.

Leningraders rushed to volunteer for the armed services during the first few days of the war. But it soon became clear, with the Panzer divisions tearing through the country, that the defence of the city itself was to be their major priority.

On 27th June the Executive Committee of the City Soviet – the council – issued an order by which everybody was called up for defence work. Only the elderly, workers in vital industries and those who were ill, pregnant or caring for small children were exempt. Those who did not have jobs were to work eight hours a day, and workers and students were to help for three hours a day when they had finished working. There was to be a four-day rest period after every seven days' work. With the fall of Pskov on 8th July the prospect for Leningrad worsened. Now people were to be given one day off after seven at work, or two days a fortnight if they were working outside the city limits.

The enemy advance continued. Admittedly, it was not progressing according to Hitler's schedule. He had planned to take the city in July, but it was September by the time the Wehrmacht reached the outskirts. The closer it got to Leningrad, the stiffer the resistance it encountered. Nevertheless, it pushed on relentlessly.

By the beginning of September the Germans were between twelve and twenty miles from the city, and were finding it difficult to advance further. On 8th September they captured Schlusselburg, east of Leningrad, on the shores of Lake Ladoga. With the assistance of the Finns to the north, the Germans had now surrounded the city. Rather than engage in costly street fighting, Hitler decided to besiege the city, strangling it with hunger and destroying it with artillery bombardment.

The Soviet Eighth Army held out at Oranienbaum, fifteen miles from Leningrad, until January 1944. But it was never able to break through the German lines to reach the city. The people of Leningrad did what they could to defend their city. They worked for twelve to sixteen hours a day, digging 626 kilometres of anti-tank ditches, putting up 50,000 concrete blocks, 626 kilometres of barbed wire entanglements and 15,000 pillboxes, and building 22,000 gun emplacements. Every street corner was turned into a defensive position, manned by machine-gunners. The city provided ten volunteer divisions and 300,000 people joined the People's Militia, known as the Opolchenie.

The Nevsky Prospekt after the bombardment of Leningrad.

Three million people were trapped inside the city. There were about 200,000 soldiers, apart from the Opolchenie, but they had only limited supplies of weapons and ammunition. Before the war Leningrad had imported most of its food and wood and all of its coal, oil, iron, steel and cotton. Only a few vegetables, some dairy products, peat and some firewood was available locally. It was clear that the city could not survive for long. The world waited, helplessly, for Leningrad to fall.

Food and fuel stocks were shrinking fast. From 1st September, blue- and white-collar workers were issued with 600 and 400 grams (1lb 6oz and 14oz) of bread a day, dependants and children, 300 grams (11oz). The authorities had calculated that there was barely enough food to last until the end of the month. Then, on the night of 8th September, the Badaev food warehouses were hit by incendiary bombs and burnt to the ground. The amount of food destroyed in this raid was exaggerated in early accounts of the siege. Total losses were probably only about 3,000 tons of flour and 2,500 tons of sugar, some of which was salvaged and used to make sweets. But it was undoubtedly demoralizing for a city facing starvation to have the night air filled with the sickly smell of burning sugar and wheat. On 10th September the rations were cut: blue-collar workers received 500 grams (1lb 2oz) of bread a day, white-collar workers 300 grams (11oz) and dependants and children 250 grams (9oz).

On 11th September, electricity was rationed for the first time. From then on, most people could use electricity for a few hours only each day, often at inconvenient times such as late at night or during the afternoon when everyone was at work. All unnecessary private telephones had already been disconnected.

At the beginning of September, the first enemy shells exploded in the streets. Although the Leningraders had known that the Germans were close, they had not realized that they were near enough to fire on the city. Soon afterwards the air-raids began. People now had to live with constant danger, and with the shrieks of air-raid sirens.

The siege of Leningrad. Map of the city inset.

But although the cold, damp winter set in, and the effects of hunger and bombardment began to take their toll, life carried on surprisingly normally in the city. Schools, factories, libraries,

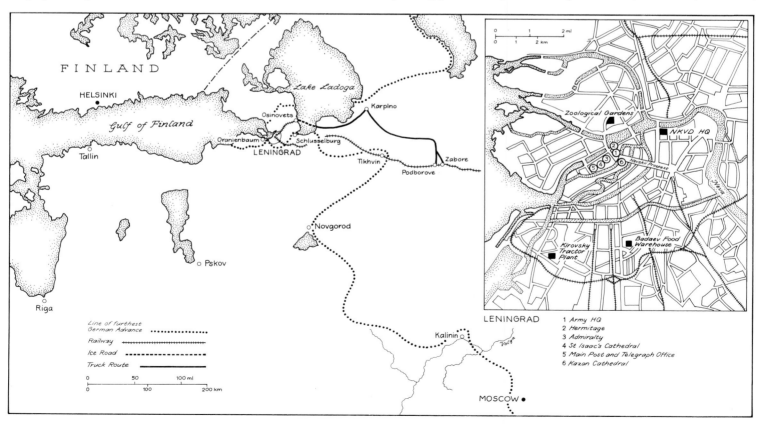

On 9th November 1941 the encirclement of Leningrad was completed. The city had enough flour for 24 days, sugar for 22 days and meat for 9 days. That evening, the Radio Symphony Orchestra, conducted by Eliasberg, performed Beethoven's Ninth Symphony at the Philharmonic Hall. The conductor later recalled the concert, which was transmitted to London:

'The concert was set for night-time. On that day the air-raid alarm was sounded eleven or twelve times. . . . Domestic broadcasts were interrupted during air-raids but not the foreign service broadcasts. The musicians who had not come well in advance of the scheduled concert had to get there as best they could at the risk of their lives.

The concert began on schedule. Two parts of the symphony were played without interruption. When the third began, we heard the wail of the sirens and almost immediately the impact of bombs falling nearby, and the thunder of anti-aircraft guns. The building shook. To that accompaniment the orchestra played the symphony to the end. The announcer signed off and wished our listeners in Great Britain goodnight.'

orchestras and cinemas remained working. Leningrad had always had a large number of active Party members. About 15% of the population, before the war, belonged to the Party itself, or to the Komsomol, the Young Communist League. Experienced Party agitators visited almost every organization, teaching the population how to cope with the difficult conditions and attempting, successfully it appears, to maintain public morale.

Repeated attempts to break through the German blockade had failed. By October, Moscow was in danger, and the Leningraders knew that if the capital were to fall, there would be little hope for them. A month later, the Germans took Tikhvin, in their attempt to control the whole of the eastern shore of Lake Ladoga. Until then, most of the supplies that had been reaching the besieged city had been brought by boat across the lake. If the Germans controlled Ladoga, Leningrad would not be able to hold out for much longer. As it was, the lake was beginning to freeze, and fewer and fewer boats were getting through. Some food was brought in to the city by air, but the Red Air Force simply did not have the planes available to maintain an adequate and regular supply. On 12th November the Leningrad newspapers and radio issued this warning: 'The Leningraders have suffered much during the months of the siege, but ahead of them are even more severe trials, even greater privations. One must be ready for them. One must look the truth straight and soberly in the face.'

From 20th November workers received 250 grams (9oz) of bread a day. Everyone else was given 125 grams (4½oz). There was almost no other food available by then. Leningrad bread, in November 1941, was made from 10% cellulose (originally intended for paper production), 10% cotton-seed oil cake (originally intended as fuel for ships' furnaces), 2% chaff, 2% flour sweepings, 3% corn flour and 73% rye flour. Industrial oils were refined for human consumption. The floorboards of breweries were lifted so that any malt could be salvaged.

At this time the city was being bombarded for an average of nine hours a day. But this was not enough to distract people from the search for food. There are reports of Leningraders boiling up old belts in the hope of extracting some nourishment from the leather, and of others trying to eat glue. A dog or a cat was worth a month's salary on the black market. Money no longer had any real value. Food was the only thing that counted. Unless a means of supply throughout the winter could be found, the city could not keep going even at this desperate level.

Andrei Zhdanov, the chairman of the Executive Committee of the City Soviet and a member of

German machine-gunners in trenches outside Leningrad.

the Military Council of the Leningrad Front, is generally believed to have masterminded the plans for the 'Lifeline Road' across the ice of Lake Ladoga. According to the experts Zhdanov consulted, the ice would not be thick enough to support vehicles until the middle of December. But Leningrad could not hold out that long, so on 18th November a reconnaissance party set out on the eighteen-mile journey over the ice on foot. They made it. The next day, work began on the ice road. It was estimated that with everyone working flat out it would take fifteen days to construct the ice road and the 352 kilometres (220 miles) of road that would be needed to join the eastern shore of Lake Ladoga with the nearest railway stations in Russian hands. This track would have to pass through a wilderness of swamps and forests.

On 20th November horse-drawn sledges began to cross the ice. The road on the other side of the lake was not yet finished, so the sledges had to make their way to the railway as best they could. Some of the horses were so enfeebled by starvation that they could not make the journey. The drivers slaughtered them on the spot, cut them up and sent the meat back to the city.

The first trucks attempted the crossing on 22nd November. Some of them fell through the ice, but the next day the survivors brought 33 tons of food back with them. The next day only 19 tons arrived. Nevertheless, the opening of the road gave people hope.

The recapture of Tikhvin, a couple of days after the successful counter-attack outside Moscow, further encouraged the Leningraders. The supply road could now be considerably shortened. On 22nd December, 700 tons of provisions were brought over the ice. The Germans bombed and strafed the road constantly. Drivers got lost in blizzards and trucks fell through bomb craters in the ice. A great many people were needed to load the trucks, control the traffic and build bridges over the holes and weak patches in the ice. Despite all the effort that was being put into operating the ice road, the people of Leningrad were dying from cold and starvation.

Suddenly, on 25th December, the bread ration was increased, giving workers an extra 100 grams (4oz) – they now received 350 grams (12oz). Everyone else found that they had an extra 75 grams (3oz), making a total of 200 grams (7oz). The increase had a remarkable effect on the population. Strangers congratulated each other and enthusiastically discussed their hopes for further increases. Two further additions to the ration meant that by the end of February food allocations were nearly as generous as they had been at the beginning of the siege.

Despite this, January and February 1942 was the worst period of the war for Leningrad. During these two months nearly 200,000 people died of cold and hunger, many of them in the streets or at their factory benches. Whole families were found together, dead, in flats which were freezing cold. Often the surviving members of a family would not have the strength to take the dead to the cemetery. Friends would say a final goodbye to each other whenever they met – they never knew who would be alive tomorrow, or next week. Yet still attempts were being made to carry on with life as usual. In January a writers' conference went ahead, even though the writers had to burn their chairs to keep warm.

Water and sewage pipes froze. There was no electricity and the public address system often broke down. There was no public transport either. Komsomol and Red Cross workers tried to locate and assist those in the greatest need. But the cold and its devastating effects went on. During January the authorities speeded up the evacuation of people whose presence in Leningrad was not essential, using the 'Lifeline Road'. Many were unwilling to go. Some were afraid of the dangers of the ice road and of German artillery. Others insisted that they simply wanted to stay in their city.

Life became a little easier for those who remained, as the ice road became more efficient, and as the evacuation reduced the number of mouths to be fed. But there was great apprehension about what would happen when the ice melted. On 15th April, the day that the last truck crossed the frozen lake, 3,000 people died in Leningrad. That same day, passers-by burst into tears and cheered at the sight of a tram running in the streets of the city. Some electricity had become available, due to locally dug peat and imported fuel. There was still none for civilians, but a limited amount of power was available for industry and public transport.

The thaw was a mixed blessing. Sewage and water-pipes that had been frozen now burst. As the ice began to melt, festering piles of rubbish were revealed. Among these were dead bodies that had been lying on the streets for weeks. The surviving population, debilitated as they were, were mobilized to clean up the city. Rations dropped temporarily with the closure of the ice road, but as soon as boats could cross the lake they were restored.

During the spring the City Soviet organized the production of vegetables wherever possible. Families, schools, factories, and offices were allocated a copy of the *Siege Gardening Handbook*, packets of seeds and plots of land. The campaign was not as successful as it might have been. Inevitably, inexperienced urban gardeners weeded up the vegetables that they had planted. There were not enough tools, nor was there enough water. But the vegetables that were grown significantly improved the Leningraders' diet during the last few months of 1942, even if they did have to pick the shrapnel out of their home-grown cabbages.

In May 1942 fresh troops crossed Lake Ladoga to strengthen the exhausted garrison. At the same time it was decided to turn Leningrad into a fortress city. Further evacuation of civilians was ordered and new defences were built inside and outside the city. Although heavy bombardment continued throughout the year, these fortifications were not put to the test because no major assault on Leningrad took place.

The winter of 1942/3 did not see a repetition of the horrors of the year before. This time, fuel supplies were built up during the summer, partly through the organized demolition of abandoned wooden houses. Everything possible was done in advance to insulate buildings against the cold. Windows were boarded up, pipes lagged with newspaper, and so on. People living on the upper storeys of apartment houses were told to move into empty flats on the first three floors.

On 18th January 1943 the Red Army established a narrow corridor linking Leningrad with the rest of the unoccupied territory. The arrival of the first train on 7th February was greeted with delight. The population assumed that the siege was over. But the Germans were still surrounding most of the city, and throughout 1943 they increased their artillery attacks.

It was not until 27th January 1944 that the enemy was finally forced to retreat all along the Leningrad front. For 900 days the city had held out against Nazi bombardment. It is not known how many people died during the siege, but it is reliably estimated at about a million.

MIG 3s patrolling the skies over Leningrad. In the foreground is the spire of the Peter Paul fortress.

Facing page: *A museum curator taking her turn firewatching on the roof of the Hermitage.*

'Citizens! During artillery fire this is the most dangerous side of the street' – a notice on the wall in the Palace Square, in front of the Winter Palace. Notice that the Alexander Andrisky column is encased in a protective structure to prevent it collapsing during bombardment.

In the Leningrad Public Library. Behind the reader, who is wearing a hat and heavy overcoat for warmth even though he is indoors, the sign reads, 'Please Keep Quiet'. But, it has been estimated, a bomb or a shell could be heard falling in the city every three minutes.

Nevsky Prospekt during shelling.

Multiple Maxim machine-guns in an anti-aircraft role, firing tracer bullets during a night raid over Leningrad.

The Hermitage Museum damaged by German shelling. In Leningrad, as elsewhere in Russia, little respect was shown by the enemy for the architectural glories of Russia's past. Tsarskoe Selo, a royal palace south of the city, was destroyed by the retreating Germans.

Women queuing for their bread ration. In December 1941, manual workers received 250 grams (9 oz) of bread daily, office workers, dependants and children 125 grams (4½ oz). Often these meagre rations could not be honoured. In Moscow, where rations were over twice as generous, the black market price for a loaf of bread was almost half the average monthly wage.

Facing page: *A delivery of bread to a shop. This photograph was evidently taken during the first winter of the siege – later on the horses pulling the cart would have been eaten.*

The bakeries of Leningrad used to burn wood from bombed houses. There were many wooden houses in the suburbs of Leningrad. When the water-mains stopped working, 8,000 Young Communist League members formed a human chain and passed water from hand to hand from the river Neva to the bakery.

'*Mummy,
We come here every day with Dad at 10 o'clock to wait for you.   Slava*'
(scrawled on a wall of the family's ruined house).

There was no heating in most of the munitions factories – the roof of this one had been blown off. Many workers slept at the plants – they did not have the energy to walk all the way home to flats that were also freezing cold.

A factory worker and member of a civilian defence unit. Workers of the Izhorsky engineering plant on the outskirts of Leningrad formed such a unit and managed to defend their factory against the Germans. The wall behind him shows the scars of fighting.

Facing page: There was no running water in Leningrad during the siege. There was no fuel to pump it and the pipes were frozen, so people had to fetch water from the river Neva, digging through several feet of ice if necessary. Even after it had been strained through eight layers of gauze, the water still tasted dreadful. Mothers with babies were naturally desperate for water, and would sometimes collect ice to wash clothes and nappies in, rather than carry every drop from the river. But even this was difficult because there was no fuel with which to melt the ice.

The Kirovsky Tractor
Plant was converted
during the war into a
tank factory, where new
tanks were built and
damaged ones repaired.

Facing page: Mechanics
driving newly built T34
tanks along Kirovsky
Prospekt to the front, a
mile or so down the road
from the factory. It was
possible to go to the front
by tram until the winter
of 1941. The trams
started again in the
summer of 1943 when an
electric cable had been
laid across the bottom of
Lake Ladoga.

Boys of thirteen or
fourteen in a munitions
factory, assembling large-
calibre shells.

98

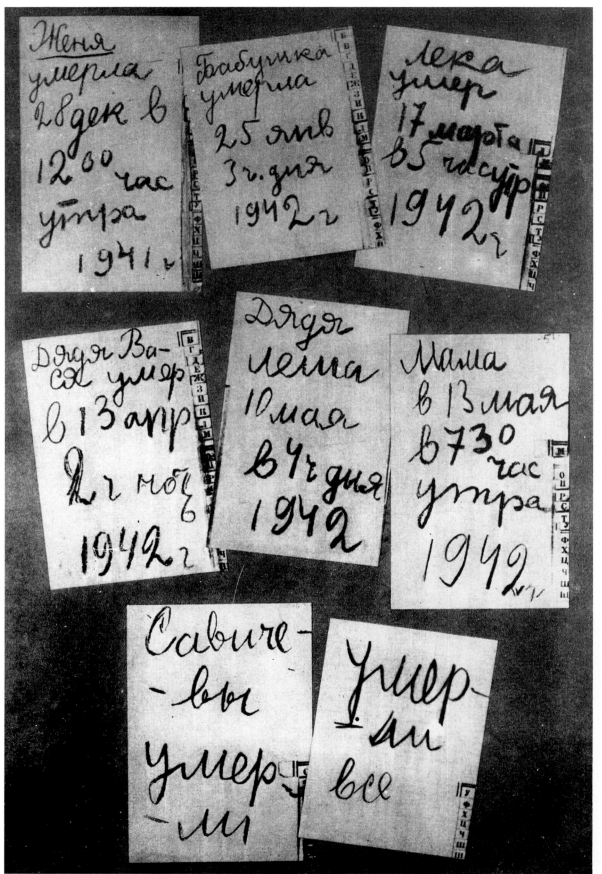

The last few pages from the diary of Tania Savicheva, a little girl living in Leningrad during the siege:
'Zhenya died 28 Dec. at 12.00, 1941.
Granny died 25 Jan. 3 in the afternoon, 1942.
Leka died 17 March at 5 morn 1942.
Uncle Vasya died 13 Apr. 2 at night, 1942.
Uncle Lyosha 10 May at 4 afternoon. 1942.
Mummy 13 May at 7.30 morning 1942.
The Savichevs are dead. All dead.'

During the siege 900,000 citizens died, a third of Leningrad's pre-1941 population, mostly from starvation. They resorted to all kinds of desperate measures in order to fill their stomachs – catching crows or rooks, or any cats and dogs which might somehow have survived; rooting through medicine chests in search of castor oil, hair oil, vaseline or glycerine; making soup or jelly out of carpenters' glue.

November 1941
When a meagre ration was introduced in the besieged city, people rushed to buy up everything that could serve as food. Pepper, ascorbic acid, powder for making *kvas*, a Russian soft drink, ginger, vanilla powder – all those spices and other things disappeared with lightning speed from the counters.

I saw a long line of people buying tablets for bad breath at a pharmacy. Surprised, I asked what people wanted them for. I was told that the tablets had a sweet taste . . . Sweet cough drops, lotions, valerian drops, peach stone oil and algae, believed to be good for atherosclerosis patients, are now used for making borshch . . . no, *were* used, I should say. All that is a thing of the past. The pharmacies are now empty.

Even though the people of Leningrad were suffering from malnutrition they responded to appeals for blood donors.

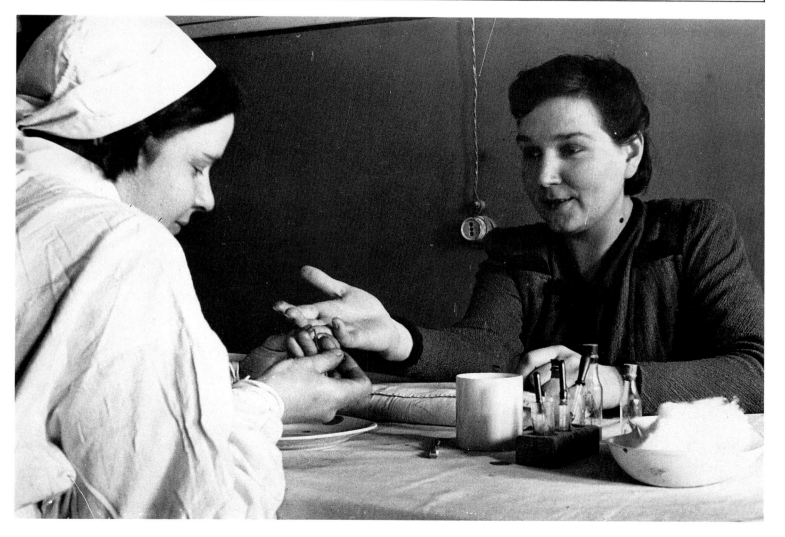

The icy streets of Leningrad were lethally dangerous. No one had the time or the strength to clear the pavements. In addition, there was the hazard of German artillery fire, particularly in the modern, southern parts of the city.

It was not uncommon during the siege for people literally to drop dead in the streets. People sitting down and resting, weakened by hunger and exhaustion, would often freeze to death.

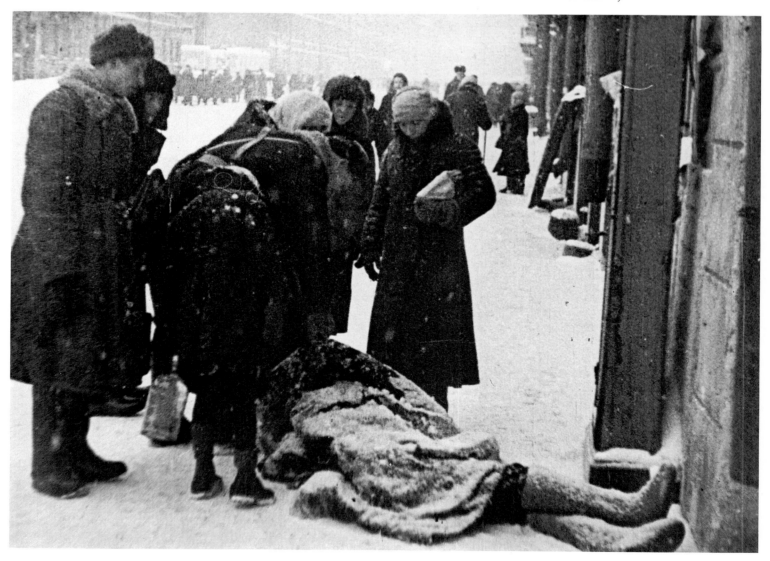

A funeral cortège crossing the Kirovsky Bridge, on the way to the Piskarov cemetery, about 6 kilometres (4 miles) away. Throughout most of the siege, people had to be buried in mass graves. These graves were made by dynamiting a hole in the ground. The cemetery guards could be bribed to dig individual graves, but they had to be paid with bread.

A patient is taken to hospital on a sledge. The people of Leningrad died of malnutrition and the cold, but they were lucky that there were no outbreaks of typhoid or dysentery, and the number of cases of influenza was below average.

Leningrad harbour, frozen up in the spring of 1942. Anti-aircraft guns were mounted on the ships, and on one ship there was an electricity generator that enabled Leningrad radio to carry on broadcasting throughout the siege, 24 hours a day. Between programmes, the radio broadcast the ticking of a metronome, to remind people that the city was alive. People who lived through the siege still shudder with horror at the sound of a metronome.

In the centre of the photograph is the famous cruiser Aurora, whose guns signalled the opening of the Bolshevik Revolution, 7th November 1917.

A Soviet naval patrol on night sentry duty.

Facing page: *The* Aurora *cruiser despite its age took part in the defence of the city. In the foreground there are 85mm anti-aircraft guns, model 1939; the shells weighed 9.2 kilograms (20.29 lb).*

The Soviet destroyer Opytnyi, *cut off in Leningrad, contributes its guns to the city's defence.*

Driver Ivan Maximov was one of the blockade runners who freighted goods to, and evacuated people from, Leningrad along the Lifeline Road from the first day to the last. He recalls:

'In the early hours of 22nd November, the first column of ten vehicles descended onto the ice from the western shore. I was with that column. A dark and windy night shrouded the lake. There was no snow yet and the black-lined field of ice looked for all the world like open water. I must admit that an icy fear gripped my heart. My hands shook, no doubt from strain and also from weakness – we had been eating a rusk a day for four days . . . but our column was fresh from Leningrad and we had seen people starving to death. Salvation was there on the eastern shore. And we knew we had to get there at any cost.

Not all the vehicles got to the other shore. But the first group crossing had been made. I even remember the taste of the first hot plate of soup we were given.'

Lorries on one of the 'lifeline roads' across Lake Ladoga. On the outward journey, shown here, the trucks carried evacuees; they returned loaded with meat, coal and flour.

The ice of the lake was riddled with bomb craters, pot-holes and damaged, abandoned vehicles. The Germans continually bombarded the roads.

This photograph was evidently taken in the spring, when the ice had begun to melt, because the truck is partly submerged.

Women and children preparing to be evacuated across Lake Ladoga. Until 22nd January 1942, women and children, old and sick people were given priority, after which time evacuation began in earnest. Between January and April, 512,000 people were evacuated; a further 449,000 were evacuated between May and November, when shipping on the lake had been restored.

June 1942

There was a young woman with twins living with me in the same house. That first winter of the blockade they were both dying. She too was not long for this world. She looked weak, lost and alone with her dependant's ration card.

One day she made a decision . . . I don't even know what to call it – a crime or a feat of bravery? No, those words are all wrong . . . Perhaps the right words don't even exist in any human language. She realized that she would not be able to save both her sons. So she stopped feeding one of them and he died.

The second pulled through though. I saw him yesterday. He was walking about the yard. A thin, pale and sad-looking boy, but he was alive . . .

A detachment of women in the 'Home Guard' marching past the Winter Palace just after the German invasion.

The alcoholics died out very fast. Misers, who'd been hoarding money for years and stinting on food, people with a passion for acquisition also met their end quickly. All too often their greed got the better of them, even on the brink of death. There was a carpenter who left behind many valuable silver and gold objects, and in his cupboard there were tins of food and two kilograms of lard. To think he had starved to death!

I try not to think of the food of former days. I forbid myself to do so. But sometimes imagination, that cur, breaks loose and then there's the devil to pay. It paints pictures of good food – rich, succulent, crisp and fried golden. Who can understand the ravings of a Leningrad citizen, the torment caused by memories of choice morsels we had left uneaten?

I recall shop-counters groaning with huge pink sausages wrapped in white fat, I recall joints of ham, garlands of frankfurters, the cool yellow cubes of butter, bottles with bright coloured labels . . .

Why did I buy no more than a hundred grams that time? Why didn't I buy, why didn't I eat, why didn't I guzzle all that? I could have, easily!

September 1942. Picking cabbages next to St Isaac's Cathedral. In the spring of 1942 there were a great many cases of scurvy in the city, so the authorities decided to use every piece of available land for growing vegetables, especially carrots and cabbages. As the siege progressed Leningraders also became more resourceful in finding other sources of vitamins. There are reports of people drinking an extract of pine needles, and water in which the bark of oak trees had been boiled – this was said to prevent stomach disorders.

Stalingrad

After its armies' ignominious defeat outside Moscow the German High Command ordered greater mobilization. It despatched another thirty-nine divisions, six brigades, about 800,000 troops in all, to reinforce its battered divisions on the Eastern Front. Hitler was determined to launch a major offensive in Russia as soon as the ground was firm enough for his Panzer divisions to roll.

Army Group North was ordered to take Leningrad, and the Central Front was to hold fast. The south was to be the main theatre of operations in the summer campaign. Here, there was to be a breakthrough to the Volga and the Caucasus. The Germans were always seeking oil. The whole war was being waged by combustion engines, and the Third Reich depended on synthetic production and what came out of the large Rumanian and Hungarian fields. The Caucasus produced three-quarters of Russia's oil, a great deal of iron ore and some coal. These mineral resources would make Hitler's aims a great deal easier to achieve, and he hoped that by depriving Russia of them, he could bring her to her knees.

The campaign opened in June. Army Group South was to capture the Crimea. Then the town of Voronezh was to be taken in a typical Panzer pincer movement. The Germans were to cross the Kerch straits into the north-west Caucasus. Then, armies coming from Dnepropetrovsk and Voronezh were to advance upon the Caucasus to seize the oil wells, at the same time throwing out a strong flank guard towards Stalingrad.

The defenders of Sebastopol were more resilient than Hitler had expected, but otherwise his campaign appeared to be a success. The Soviet Union was losing more and more of its territory. Red Army counter-attacks had driven the Germans back about 320 kilometres (200 miles) in some places, but on the whole they had not been successful. There were heavy casualties, and an attempt to recapture Kharkov in May resulted in the loss of three armies, four generals and a quarter of a million prisoners.

Voronezh fell on 6th July and the drive on the Caucasus and Stalingrad began. Suddenly Hitler amended his strategy. He abandoned the idea of conquering the south step by step. Instead, he decided to launch simultaneous attacks on Stalingrad and the Caucasus. The German generals protested, to no avail, and the campaign went ahead.

Rostov was taken on 23rd July. Despite the German successes, the Red Army was no longer losing large numbers of men. Stalin had learnt that it was better to allow his armies to melt away as the Germans approached, rather than to risk losing valuable manpower and equipment.

Hitler changed his mind again. He ordered the Fourth Panzer Army, which had been part of the assault on the Caucasus, to swing round and join the Sixth Army in the attack on Stalingrad.

In the trenches, Stalingrad. There was a saying in Red Army barracks: 'If you don't die during your first battle you'll survive.'

He also detached a considerable portion of the artillery that had been on the road to the Caucasus and sent it up to Leningrad.

The army that faced Stalingrad was, therefore, weaker than it need have been. But it still consisted of about 400,000 men. By 23rd August, Colonel-General Friedrich Paulus and his Sixth Army were on the left bank of the Volga, north of Stalingrad, and were advancing into the suburbs. That day, every available plane on the Russian front bombarded the city. Over 600 planes were involved in the raids, which killed 40,000 civilians and wounded 150,000. Afterwards, the city was reported to be a blazing inferno, with oil tanks throwing up columns of flame 200 metres (650ft) high. The evacuation of the civilian population began in earnest after 23rd August.

Hitler was obsessed with Stalingrad; he saw the battle for the city as a personal duel with the Russian leader. Stalin was equally determined that the city named after him should not fall into German hands. The city had originally been called Tsaritsyn, the 'Tsarina's City'. It had been an important trading post since the sixteenth century, because of its strategic position as the gateway both to the Caucasus and to the eastern territories. In the autumn of 1918 Stalin led the defence of the city against the advancing White Guard troops, and so in 1925 the city was renamed Stalingrad in honour of this successful stand. By 1939 it had a population of 445,000, and included several industrial complexes that were of major importance to the war effort. The country's first tractor plant, the Krasnii Oktyabr iron and steel plant and the Barrikadi machine-building plant were all built there. The city was a most unusual shape. By the beginning of the war it was twenty miles long, but only three miles wide at its broadest point. It was built along the high western bank of the Volga, with only a very small extension on the eastern side of the river.

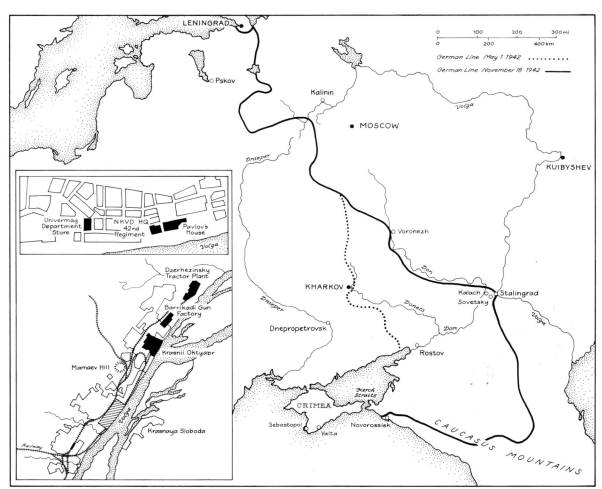

Stalingrad, showing the extent of the German penetration, 18th November 1942. Map of the city inset.

The dead Red Army crew of a Maxim 7.62mm PM 1910 machine-gun of the Sokolov type in a trench outside Stalingrad.

By 2nd September Paulus had seized control of the area between the Don and the Volga and had joined up with the Fourth Panzer Army. Tanks and infantry began to advance towards the city centre. The Germans, used to the continual Soviet withdrawals of the past few months, were confident. They thought that Russian reserves of matériel, manpower and morale were exhausted. But although the Red Army had been driven back into the centre of Stalingrad, it was standing its ground. No sooner had the Germans taken possession of a street, or a building, than they found themselves under attack again. The Russian troops were relentless. They fought in the factories, in the ruins of buildings and even in the sewers. General Chuikov, the Red Army Commander, knew that the Germans could not bear close fighting. His order to the troops was 'We should get as close to the enemy as possible, so that his air force cannot bomb our forward units or trenches. Every German soldier must be made to feel that he is living under the muzzle of a Russian gun.'

The fighting was so heavy that in September, although it was still summer, every leaf had fallen from the trees. A BBC broadcast from London on 11th October described the battle raging in Stalingrad: 'The Germans themselves now call Stalingrad the Russian Verdun. But Verdun was a fortress. Stalingrad is an open city. . . This is not a battle for a locality or a river, but for street crossings and houses. Stalingrad has defeated Hitler's armies. Poland was conquered in 28 days. In 28 days in Stalingrad the Germans took several houses. France was defeated in 38 days. In Stalingrad it took the Germans 38 days to advance from one side of the street to the other.'

By 11th November, Soviet troops were just managing to hold on to a thin strip of territory on the river banks to the south of the city, on Mamaev Hill and in a few isolated pockets elsewhere in the city. The most renowned of the strongholds of Russian resistance was a badly damaged apartment house facing Solechnaya Street. On 28th September Sergeant Jacob Pavlov and three others crawled across a courtyard towards the house, and threw hand grenades in through the window. As a handful of Germans ran for cover elsewhere Pavlov's group dived into the ground floor rooms. They found several Russians in the basement, some of them badly wounded. The next day a messenger managed to get through to Headquarters, and 'Dom Pavlov', 'Pavlov's House', became a crucial fortification and landmark on all HQ maps. The squat, simple peasant Pavlov, codenamed 'Lighthouse', defended his house with ferocity and cunning for 58 days. He and his friends found a gramophone in their house, and one record, which they played until it wore out. It was not a tune they recognized, but it kept them going as they faced constant artillery and even tank attacks.

Miraculously, in the middle of November the shipbuilding works was still repairing tanks and a local power plant was still producing electricity.

While Chuikov had the desperate task of trying to organize an army scattered among the rubble that had once been Stalingrad, Marshal Zhukov, on the far side of the Volga, was planning a counter-attack. He was amassing a huge force of twelve armies and was relying on the coming winter to help him.

The Soviet counter-attack on 19th November took the Germans by surprise. It immediately routed their allied Rumanian troops to the north-west of the city. The next day, a hundred miles to the south, the Red Army overran a mixed German and Rumanian force. The two Soviet armies joined up on 22nd November. Paulus and the Sixth Army were completely cut off.

It was not until 31st January that Friedrich Paulus emerged from his HQ in the basement of the Univermag department store, to surrender what was left of his army – 91,000 officers and men. German troops ironically called their brief campaign the 'Caucasus Round Trip'. The German invasion had lasted six months, from August 1942 to January–February 1943. The humiliating German evacuation of the Caucasus was a direct result of the encirclement of the Sixth Army at Stalingrad and the subsequent re-capture of the Don country by the Russians.

Most of the buildings of Stalingrad lay in ruins. In May, four months after the end of the battle, the task of rebuilding the city began. By September the population had swelled to 210,000 and by May 1945 90% of its industrial capacity was operative again.

Even before Paulus surrendered, the German drive on the Caucasus had been halted.

A moment of rest in the trenches outside Stalingrad.

September 1942. The last desperate Soviet attempt to smash through the German armies surrounding Stalingrad looked for a moment as though it might succeed. Ten tanks broke through the enemy lines and reached the city. But the Germans soon closed in behind them.

The steppes surrounding Stalingrad are flat, open grassland. There are no fences or hills, and few trees or buildings to provide cover.

A duel between two Soviet soldiers, manning a 14.5mm anti-tank rifle PTRS 1941, and a German tank.

A war reporter interviewing a soldier in the trenches near Stalingrad. The gun in the foreground is a Degtyarev 7.62mm DP 1928 machine-gun.

Some of the most bitter fighting in Stalingrad was for the Dzerhezinsky Tractor Plant in the north of the city. Since the German invasion the factory had become one of the biggest producers of T-34 tanks in the country. In August, under artillery fire, it built nearly 400 tanks. The same month, the workers of the plant, and of every other factory in Stalingrad, were organized into a Workers' Militia. Everyone who enlisted was given a red armband, a rifle and a bandolier of ammunition.

In October when German soldiers reached the Tractor Plant, they met strong resistance. One of the toughest defenders of the factory was Olga Kovalova, a foul-mouthed veteran who had worked with the men in the plant for 20 years, and had become Russia's first woman steel founder. Her battalion commander tried to get rid of her, insisting that it was no place for a woman. But she stayed, and continued to bawl out any of the men that she considered lazy or ineffective. After the attack she was found dead.

By 18th October the Germans had captured the Tractor Plant. Here, in the final stages of the battle for the factory, it is clear that it has been reduced to a pile of rubble, and a tangle of girders and wrecked machinery.

Three months later the Tractor Plant was to be the final bolt-hole for the Germans in Stalingrad. After Field Marshal Paulus had surrendered on 31st January 1943, General Karl Strecker and the remnants of the 11th Corps held out here for another two days.

In the trenches a Red Army soldier checks his 7.62mm PPSh 1941 submachine-gun. It operated on the same blowback principle as other Soviet submachine-guns, and was fed from a drum magazine based on the famous Thompson machine-gun used by gangsters. The barrels were mainly salvaged from quantities of obsolete M1891 rifles, each barrel providing two submachine-gun barrels. The barrels were chromed and therefore did not need frequent cleaning. The magazine held 70 rounds, and could be emptied in just over 30 seconds.

It was a cheap and easy gun to produce, simple to maintain and reliable. It could be dragged through mud, immersed in water or left out in snow and ice without being damaged.

Soldiers and workers' militiamen unloading ammunition from a barge. After 18th September, when a large quantity of ammunition for the 13th Guards had been blown up on the river-bank, all goods being unloaded had to be taken to specially prepared caches nearby. In practice, ammunition was almost always taken straight to the front, a few streets away. Any available craft was used to ferry troops and ammunition, including little rowing-boats and inflatable dinghies. This bizarre fleet was manned by local fishermen.

Soldiers and equipment, including horses, crossing the Volga by raft.

October 1942. Stalingrad was threatened by Germans and their Rumanian allies to the north, to the south and to the west. The only hope of supplies and reinforcements lay to the east, across the river Volga. Here, a fresh infantry unit arrives, armed with submachine-guns and anti-tank guns. Ferries bringing troops into the city were bombed from the air and shelled from the German vantage points in the city; the river itself had been mined. It was not unusual for as much as half of a unit to be killed crossing the Volga.

Every ferryload of soldiers was accompanied by political commissars, responsible for ideological training, or politruk. They led the soldiers on to the boats and handed out pamphlets entitled What a Soldier Needs to Know and How to Act in City Fighting. These politruk whipped up the troops' fighting spirits and calmed them down during bombardment.

The Volga River Flotilla, formed in July 1942, consisted of armed gunboats, minesweepers and anti-aircraft gunboats. The flotilla helped with the ferrying and provided cover for the other boats working on the river. It only operated until November, when the Volga froze over, after which troops and supplies were transported over the ice, as in Leningrad.

The most brilliant snipers in the Russian and German armies were brought to Stalingrad. Endless tales – some undoubtedly apocryphal – are told of their skill, ingenuity and resilience. This photograph illustrates one of the difficulties they had to face. The lifts in many of the damaged buildings were no longer working and so the riflemen had to climb up the walls of the buildings if they wanted a good vantage point, and jump down again afterwards.

The tactics of the **Blitzkrieg**, which the Germans had previously employed so successfully, were useless in the streets of Stalingrad. Every few yards of rubble were fought for bitterly, often in hand-to-hand combat with rifle butts and bayonets. Frequently, Nazi troops would enter a building, pursued by Russians. The Germans would be driven up to the top floor, and the Russians were then frequently surrounded when another group of Germans arrived. Many buildings were taken and lost several times during the course of a few days.

Russian soldiers try to defend the ruins of a house. The soldier in the foreground is carrying a submachine-gun, and the other man is carrying a flame-thrower. Both of them are wearing protective clothing. The flame-thrower was very effective in street battles, especially against tanks.

The wounded were evacuated across the Volga, but the dead had to be buried somehow in the ruins of the city. Many bodies were lost among the rubble, or lay exposed in streets that were being fought for. Normally, there would have been special Funeral Teams whose responsibility it was to bury those killed in action, but there was no time for such niceties in Stalingrad. However, at least this commanding officer was able to give an address at the funeral of one of his men.

An old musician whose home has been destroyed in the fighting takes his most precious possession with him to safety.

In this still from a documentary film a commander is urging his men to storm a house, bringing with them enough ammunition to defend the position.

By 1942 people had discovered how to make bombs in bottles, known outside the Soviet Union as Molotov cocktails (the name dated from the Russo-Finnish War, 30th November 1939 – 13th March 1940). The bombs ignited on impact – they did not have to be lit with a match. A solution of white phosphorus and sulphur was dissolved in sulphur dioxide. The mixture burst into flames when the bottle was smashed, and burned at a temperature of 1300°C. Here, Stalingrad factory workers produce these bombs, for use against tanks.

When the fighting in Stalingrad was at its heaviest, a communications wire was hit and telephone communications broken off. Private Kitain was ordered to find the fault and mend it. He crawled under heavy fire until he found the place where the wire had been torn by a shell fragment. At that moment he was mortally wounded, but found the strength to connect the two ends of the wire with his teeth. And so he died . . . clenching the wires. The communications link was re-established.

Communications were vital as the battle raged among the ruins of Stalingrad. Pockets of Russian defenders were often surrounded by Germans; houses taken by the enemy were isolated in areas still in Russian hands. Observation posts were set up on the upper floors of buildings.

A soldier who was a watch-repairer in civilian life repairs a clock that he has found in an abandoned house.

21st September 1942

The situation in Stalingrad has become tense over the past few days. The north-western perimeter of the city is the scene of savage encounters and every street and house has turned into a battlefield. There's hand-to-hand fighting in the suburbs. The first floor of a building is often occupied by Germans while the Red Army men continue to hold the second and third floors. Floorboards are yanked up and gaps made in ceilings and walls. There is fighting in apartments and corridors.

The Germans are determined to seize Stalingrad at any cost. With continuous attacks the German Command is striving to exhaust the defenders. But the defenders' staying power is formidable.

We drew back to Stalingrad not because it was easier to defend. Our troops know what Stalingrad and the Volga mean to the country. Especially Stalingrad. But we are hard pressed. Although the Germans are suffering appalling losses, our casualties are heavy, too. We are also sustaining considerable losses in manpower and weapons. On top of everything else, this theatre of the war is a difficult one. Communications are bad, and the contours of the land are not an asset. In spite of these difficulties, not a single one of the men fighting for Stalingrad has entertained the thought of surrendering the city, of withdrawing. We want victory. Today we think of it with still greater intensity than we did two or even three weeks ago.

Soldiers in a dug-out shelter during the battle of Stalingrad. One of the most popular songs of the war was entitled In a dug-out:

'In our dug-out a log fire's aflame . . .
Weeping resin, it sputters and sighs,
The accordion's tender refrain
Sings of you and your smile and your eyes.

We are now many light years apart
And divided by snow-covered steppes
Though the road to your side is so hard,
To death's door it's an easy four steps.'

It was written in a dug-out by the war correspondent Alexei Surkov, during the battle for Moscow in late November 1941. He sent it to his wife. It was criticized by the authorities on the grounds that it was bad for morale. The last line was thought to be defeatist.

Surkov refused to rewrite it, and was supported by the men in the lines. Six soldiers in a Guards tank unit wrote to the author, saying: 'For them you say that death is four thousand English miles away but for us, leave the song as it is. We have counted the steps it takes to die.'

On a makeshift stove on a bomb-site a cook prepares kasha *(buckwheat porridge).*

A pause for a cup of tea.

All Russians know that the vital footwear for the winter are valenki – felt boots, worn with galoshes. Leather boots, even with several pairs of socks, are just not warm enough for the worst Russian cold. These straw boots, manufactured by the Germans in the occupied territories, must have been horribly inadequate. They were unkindly described by Soviet soldiers as ersatz valenki.

Cavalry units proceeding to the assembly area at the beginning of an offensive. Cavalry troops were used very little after the end of 1942. But at the outset, the Red Army was short of armoured personnel carriers, trucks and other vehicles that could cross difficult terrain. Swift cavalry battalions were therefore used to break through the enemy lines, and in attempts to encircle German troops. Germany, too, used large numbers of horses for transport on the Eastern Front, and also deployed cavalry units.

It is not easy to be the first up with a frantic 'Forward!' when your only wish, the only natural wish under the circumstances, is to dig in, to burrow as deep as possible into the earth. All around is a roar of explosions, a whining, wailing inferno, and death is hurriedly and greedily seeking you with intent to murder, perhaps slowly and painfully; your comrades are still lying pinned down to the warm earth – they will lie there motionless for another few seconds, for . . . an eternity!

That instant or two that you stand alone, you have a feeling that all the shells and mines, all the splinters and bullets are coming at you and you alone . . . After all, there seems to be no one else there to hit . . . 'My turn has come. I'm the one they're after . . .' Then, relief floods you as everyone rises – there is a slim chance there may not be enough of that stuff for all of us . . .

No, it's not at all easy to be the first up, but . . . it has to be done . . . And up you go, propelled as though by a spring. Up, together with the rocket, and your all too human fear is drowned in your hoarse 'Follow me!', and all that's left is the heat of battle and the will to win, no matter what.

On 31st January 1943, Hitler promoted Colonel-General Paulus to the rank of Field Marshal. Paulus and his staff were surrounded in their headquarters in the basement of the Univermag department store. No German Field Marshal had ever been captured alive – so the promotion was as good as an order to commit suicide. But later that day Paulus surrendered. His captor was Lieutenant Fyodor Mikhailovich Yelchenko.
   Paulus survived the war, and taught at a Soviet Military Academy afterwards. He died in 1957 in East Germany. Here, he is seen with his Chief of Staff, Lieutenant General Schmidt and A.D.C., Colonel Adam.

91,000 German soldiers and officers were captured at Stalingrad, including 24 generals. Here, a column of prisoners is being marched to a camp in the Urals.

A village near Stalingrad, liberated during the December offensive, with the whole of its surviving population. The village was overrun so quickly that the retreating Germans did not have time to burn the buildings down before they left. The tank is the famous T34.

23rd November 1942. Russian soldiers shout, embrace and dance in the snow as the two armies involved in the counterattack meet at Sovet

An aerial view of the city of Stalingrad after the battle. Stalingrad was the graveyard of over 200,000 Germans.

Right: A Stalingrad street just after the German surrender. The two cameramen are filming a documentary about the battle. In addition to the 91,000 prisoners, the Russians took 750 planes, 1,550 tanks, 480 armoured cars, 8,000 guns and mortars, 61,000 trucks, 235 munition dumps and vast quantities of other equipment.

Facing page: A Red Army soldier with a grenade, in the foreground, and two anti-tank riflemen in the ruins of Stalingrad.

The Partisans

In his famous broadcast to the nation on 3rd July 1941, Josef Stalin called upon Soviet citizens 'to establish, in the area occupied by the enemy, partisan units on foot and horseback. Moreover, bands of saboteurs must be organized to fight hostile detachments, to blow up bridges and roads, to interrupt telephone and telegraph communications and to set camps and depots on fire.' He went on: 'In the territories, insufferable conditions must be created for the enemy. You must follow him everywhere and annihilate his forces.'

Whether in response to Stalin's appeal, or to the behaviour of the Nazis, men, women and adolescents were soon rushing to enlist in the partisan movement. Barely a month after the invasion there were 200 partisan detachments or groups in the Leningrad province alone. In November 10,000 partisans took part in the Battle of Moscow. By the end of the year, 90,000 fighters were operating behind enemy lines. Some of the detachments had been organized by local Party and government bodies prior to the retreat. Others sprang up after the invasion. Throughout the occupied territory, underground Party committees, local committees and Komsomol city and district committees proliferated. But despite all this enthusiasm, the partisan movement was not well organized during the first year of the war.

There was no clear chain of command. There was a serious shortage of weapons and ammunition. There was a lack of the specialized equipment necessary for reconnaissance, communications and sabotage operations. These difficulties were exacerbated by the breakdown of administration that followed the German invasion. Small, improvised partisan units were quickly smashed by the enemy, or broken up when key members were captured or killed. Unnecessary security risks were taken. For example, too many people knew who belonged to the partisan groups, and far too many people knew the details of what they were doing. As a result, the Germans found it fairly easy to locate any potential informers and to extract information from them. Even where units were working successfully they were not as effective as they would have been had activities between different units been properly coordinated. Isolated groups of soldiers, cut off behind the German lines, often operated independently from the local partisans, and almost always without the necessary leadership.

Despite all these difficulties, even in the early stages of the war partisan operations made a significant contribution to the war effort. In two separate operations in October 1941, 1,400 Red Army soldiers stranded in the occupied territory were led back to the Russian lines with the help of partisan groups. Josef Goebbels, Hitler's Minister of Propaganda, admitted in his diaries that the resistance movement was undermining Nazi activities:

'6th March, 1942. An SD Report (Security Service of Himmler's SS) informed me about the situation in occupied Russia. It is, after all, more unstable than was generally assumed. The partisan danger is increasing week by week. The partisans are in command of large areas in occupied Russia and are conducting a régime of terror there.

A partisan reconnaissance group near Briansk. Here, the photographer was clearly a member of the partisan unit. During the 'Rail War', Briansk partisans blew up over 17,000 rails between 21st July and 27th September 1943.

Belorussian partisans wading through a marsh. The Germans marked many such marshes as impassable on their maps of this area, but the local people invariably knew of paths across them.

16th March, 1942. The activity of partisans has increased noticeably in recent weeks. They are conducting a well-organized guerrilla war. It is very difficult to get at them because they are using such terrorist methods in the areas we occupy that the population is afraid of collaborating with us any longer.

29th April, 1942. The danger of partisans in the occupied areas continues to exist in unmitigated intensity. They have caused us very great difficulties during the winter, and these are by no means finished with the coming of spring. Partisans have blasted the railway tracks in the central front between Briansk and Rosslau at five points – a further proof of their extremely discomfiting activity.'

Goebbels realized that the brutal *Untermensch* policy of men like Gauleiter Erich Koch, Reichskommissar of the Ukraine, was bound to destroy any temptation to collaborate: 'We have hit the Russians, and especially the Ukrainians, too hard . . . a clout on the head is not always a convincing argument,' he admitted.

A crucial function of the partisans was to maintain morale among the civilian population. Even though the existence of the resistance movement brought hideous reprisals upon everyone living in the occupied territories, it reminded them that the fight was going on. The Soviet Union had not surrendered. At Kiev in November 1941, for example, 800 civilians were shot for a single act of arson. Shortly afterwards, in the same city a public notice was issued which stated: 'A communications installation has been maliciously damaged. Since the perpetrators could not be traced, 400 Kiev citizens were shot.' Incidents such as these inevitably swelled the ranks of the partisans.

In May 1942 a Central Headquarters for the Partisan Movement was set up by the Stavka to take control of all resistance operations. Republican and Regional Partisan Headquarters were established, and efficient liaison between the Red Army and partisan units was organized for the first time. Training centres with Red Army and NKVD (Security Services) instructors had been set up in the autumn of 1941. Now they were expanded to give recruits, as quickly as possible, a thorough grounding in the necessary skills. These included parachuting, a knowledge of economical demolition techniques and intelligence-gathering procedure, wireless operation and the ability to forge or amend German documents when necessary for undercover work. At the same time as the Partisan Headquarters was established, Underground Party Organizations, crucial both to the armed resistance and to the maintenance of a skeleton form of Soviet Government, were being strengthened.

This was the start of the large-scale, well-coordinated partisan operations. That year, 1942, the Wehrmacht was forced to divert up to 24 divisions of its regular army to fight the partisans. But it was in the summer of 1943 that the movement had the greatest success. As the Soviet Army launched its counter-offensive with the Battle of Kursk, resistance groups mounted a concerted effort to destroy Wehrmacht communications and supply lines.

There were more than 250,000 fighters in the Partisan units by 1944. The biggest group in Belorussia, consisting of over 150,000 men, worked closely with the Red Army throughout the year. When the drive to liberate Belorussia began, they blew up more than 60,000 railway trucks, paralysing all German attempts to bring up reserves. They entered the capital of Belorussia – Minsk – together with the regular army. Minsk had been one of the first big cities to be occupied. From the outset, the Germans were given no peace. Oberst E. Westphal wrote to his brother at the front on 5th August, 1943: 'Here in Minsk we hear booming every day and at night there's firing just like in the trenches. Sometimes guns fire, or perhaps it's the damned mines. There are plenty of them here. The power station was blown up and we had no electricity for a week. On Sunday a car blew up by the officers' club and a locomotive by the water-tower. Many Germans have been shot in the streets from behind corners. I'm cracking up.'

In his semi-official history of the partisan movement B. S. Telpukhovsky claims that in three years (1941–4) the partisans of Belorussia accounted for 500,000 enemy soldiers, including 47 generals and Hitler's Reichskommissar Wilhelm Kube, who was killed by a time-bomb placed in his bed by his Belorussian mistress. In the Ukraine, according to Telpukhovsky, the partisans killed 460,000 Germans, wrecked or seriously damaged 5,000 railway engines, 50,000 railway trucks and 15,000 motor vehicles.

As the liberation of the country progressed it was no longer necessary to control all partisan activities from Moscow. In January 1944 the Stavka wound up the General Staff of the Partisan Movement. It was now more efficient for the Soviet Army to deal with and supply the units on the ground. But even after the Germans had been driven out of the Soviet Union, former partisans fought with the regular army, right up to the liberation of Berlin.

Old Bolsheviks with experience of underground work before the Revolution and during the civil war were key members of the partisan movement in many areas. Altogether more than one million partisans, men and women of all ages, fought behind the enemy lines during the war.

Partisans lay mines under the rails, having overcome the German guard patrolling the track. The Germans have cleared the land on either side of the railway to deprive the partisans of hiding places.

'To combat partisan harassment on the railways, the Germans built fortifications, laid mines around crossings, stations and bridges, and chopped down trees on both sides of the tracks. Guards mowed down people who appeared on the tracks or anywhere near them. We often watched German sappers with mine detectors and dogs moving down railway tracks, preceded by guards on both sides who also had dogs with them sometimes. What we did was to lay our mines after the guards had passed. Fooling the bloodhounds was more difficult. They had been trained to nose out tolite (a compound of TNT), so they found the mines. Then we started to divert their attention by dropping little bits of melted tolite here and there. The dogs would mistake these for mines. They would then be punished for that, and start ignoring the real mines. The Germans remarked wrily: 'The partisans have recruited our dogs.'

Farid Fazliahmetov, a partisan miner.

The people of Odessa are well known in the Soviet Union for their earthy sense of humour and vigorous language. Here is a group from the small, but important, local partisan unit. They lived in caves on the coast and managed to sabotage the enemy in the port and in the shipyards where German ships were being repaired.

After the defeat of the Germans near Moscow the partisan movement grew in effectiveness. In 1942 the partisans gained control of whole regions where they managed to reintroduce Soviet rule. In Orel Province, 18,000 partisans belonging to 54 detachments controlled an area comprising 490 villages.

In this photograph, taken in 1942, a large partisan unit in Belorussia is on the march.

A German soldier in front of one of the hundreds of Russian villages which were burnt to the ground.

A great many children, like this boy, were active in the partisan movement. They were invaluable in the occupied territory because they could slip around without alerting the suspicions of the Germans.

Facing page: *Radio operators, snipers and other essential specialists parachuted into the occupied territories, usually by night. Local partisans signalled to the Russian pilots by lighting bonfires. In some areas they managed to clear areas of woodland large enough for an airstrip.*

Among the fighters who joined the partisans in this way were a number of photographers, including Boris Trachmon who took several of the photographs in this chapter. He took part in the 'Rail War' proclaimed by the Soviet Supreme Command on 14th July 1943. This was an all-out attack on vital railway lines in territory occupied by the Germans. On the night of 20th July in the Briansk, Orel and Gomel area 5,800 rails were blown up.

The aircraft shown is the Lisunov Li–2, the Soviet version of the famous Douglas DC3 Dakota, produced under licence in the USSR.

Sidor Kovpak, a former schoolteacher who had fought in the civil war and became one of the leading partisan commanders. He controlled a unit of about 10,000 men, which had its own artillery based in the nearby town of Putivt in the Ukraine. As the Germans retreated, Kovpak and his men moved ahead of them, destroying communications. They were later active in Poland.

Portraits of partisan fighters.

Destroying rail communications was a vital task for partisan units. In Belorussia, between August and November 1943, 200,000 rails were blown up, 1,014 trains were wrecked or derailed, 814 locomotives were wrecked or damaged, and 72 railway bridges were destroyed or damaged.

Explosives experts parachuted into the occupied territory to train local partisans to handle and manufacture bombs. Here, a partisan, armed with a Schmeisser sub-machine-gun stolen from the German army, lights the fuse of a bomb planted on a main railway line.

A partisan base in the woods. The partisans could rarely light bonfires, because of the risk that the Germans would see the smoke and track them down.

In the autumn of 1942, the Briansk Front Headquarters received a radio message: 'We have weapons. If necessary we can seize more from the enemy. What we need is a song. We cannot get one as a trophy. Send us a song.' It was signed by the Partisans of the Briansk Forest. The poet Antolii Sofronov and composer Sigizmund Katz found it difficult to decide what sort of song to write. It could not be a marching song – partisans do not march. They do not sing loudly, either. The less they are seen and heard the better. The result was an epic song in the old Russian tradition, that could be sung very softly in chorus.

It was performed for the first time in a dug-out on the night of 6th November 1942, at a party to celebrate the 25th anniversary of the October Revolution:

'The Briansk Forest
  murmured grimly
As the blue fog settled
  down
The pines all around
  strained to hear
The tread,
The tread of partisans
  going into battle. . .'

In the Autumn of 1942 we learned that the Germans were preparing a punitive operation against our partisan unit. The bridge across a nearby river had to be blown up so the tanks and armoured personnel carriers would not get through. But the bridge was closely guarded. My 12-month-old daughter was with me in the partisan hideout and when I went scouting I always left her with my mother who was with us there. On learning that several attempts to mine the bridge had failed I went to the commander and volunteered to do the job. I wrapped the small but powerful time-bomb in a bundle with my daughter, took a basketful of apples and set out for the market in the nearby village. The way to the market lay across the bridge. The guard at one end of the bridge checked to see what was in my basket and took almost half of my apples but let me through. In the middle of the bridge I stopped to change my crying daughter's nappies . . . Swiftly and deftly I attached the mine to a girder. At the other end of the bridge the Germans checked my basket again and left me a few apples but let me go. The bridge blew up three hours later. It took the Germans a month to repair it.

Partisan life was geared to long spells in the woods, where many of the comforts of city life were lacking. Nevertheless, the partisans even put up Russian bathhouses.

It was at our bathhouse that a funny thing happened one day. We had a chamber for disinfecting clothes that had been rigged up from an empty barrel. A squad of sappers returning from a mission were warned that they should remove matches from pockets before disinfecting their clothes. But no mention was made of cartridges, grenades and detonators. Off went the boys for a couple of hours of relaxation in the steam bath when they heard a burst of shots and explosions . . . The entire squad tumbled out of the bathhouse without a stitch on their backs – they were sure the Germans were attacking. Luckily their greatcoats and boots remained intact because it was winter and there was no clothing except for some captured German uniforms in the store-house.

One of the partisans, formerly a teacher of zoology, found a foolproof method for disinfecting clothes in summer. There were lots of ant-hills in the forest and it took the ants five minutes to pick clothing clean of all parasites.

German soldiers inspecting a train that has been blown up by partisans. This may have been an empty train, sent along the rails ahead of one carrying troops or ammunition. To deter partisans, the Germans would sometimes use a train full of Russian prisoners in this way.

As the Germans were forced to retreat they destroyed everything they left behind them. Here a group of German soldiers are destroying rail communications to hinder the Red Army's advance.

Zoia Kosmodemianskaia, 18 years old, a member of the Moscow Komsomol and a partisan, is escorted to her execution by German soldiers. She was caught setting light to German stables in the village of Petrischevo. Although she was tortured, the Germans did not extract any information and so she was hanged on 29th November 1941. The sign round her neck says 'She set fire to houses'.

Just before her execution she turned to a German soldier and said, 'You can't hang all 190 million of us.'

Lidin, a war reporter for Pravda, discovered the story of Zoia and saw her frozen, tortured body with the rope still round her neck, two weeks later. His story made her a national heroine and a symbol of partisan resistance.

Heinrich Himmler, Reichsführer S.S. and Chief of the German Police, inspecting a prisoner-of-war camp in occupied Russia. Most of these camps were used to assemble prisoners who were then transported to Germany as forced labour. Over 3 million Soviet prisoners died in German hands, either from starvation, neglect or sheer brutality on the part of their captors. All Jews, political commissars and Communist Party functionaries were immediately executed when they were taken prisoner.

Partisan greetings from the marshes, forests and partisan camps of Belorussia!

There's something new on every day. Sometimes we hack away so the Germans are hard pressed. Sometimes, when we're at a disadvantage – we evade combat. Lots of Nazi trains are being derailed. Sometimes we eat our fill and sleep in warmth, sometimes we go hungry for five days in a row, sometimes we're so cold our teeth chatter. There are provocateurs, and spies and traitors. Sometimes they escape retribution, but most of the time they are made to feel the accuracy of partisan bullets.

My men have played such havoc with the Germans that they drew up three divisions and combed the entire region looking for me. But we gave them a good hiding and made ourselves scarce. My head is priced pretty high as it is, but the reward goes up after every operation, of which there are many, and they are all major ones. Today the price for my head stands at 50,000 marks, an iron cross and a wonderful life back in Germany for anyone, including closest relatives, who delivers me to the German authorities dead or alive.

The execution of young members of the Minsk underground, autumn 1941. It is estimated that well over a million people had been slaughtered in Belorussia, of which Minsk is the capital, during the German occupation. This included the entire Jewish population and many thousands of partisans and their 'helpers', among them women and children.

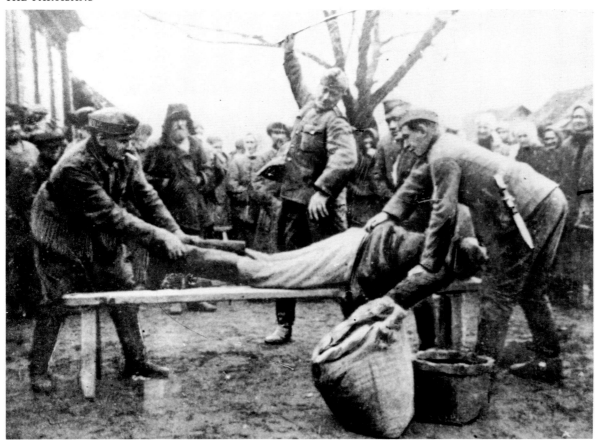

From the start, the Germans were much more brutal in Russia than in the countries they occupied in Western Europe. Here, German soldiers beat a peasant who has refused to hand over food supplies to them.

The execution of Russian partisans. The Germans shot or hanged all Communist Party Members, including Young Communists. German atrocities inevitably strengthened the resistance movement. In Belorussia, in February 1943, for example, there were 65,000 armed partisans; by December there were 360,000.

At first the Germans tried to entice people into going to work in Germany. When this failed, they transported civilians to work as slave labourers, in factories, on farms or as domestic servants. The deportees had to wear a distinguishing badge with the legend OST (East). Nearly 4 million **Ostarbeiter** (east workers) from the Soviet Union – most of them from the Ukraine – were deported as slave labour to the Reich.

Farm produce from Belorussia being loaded onto a train bound for Germany. This consignment appears to be boxes of eggs, but butter, meat, potatoes and other vegetables were also exported.

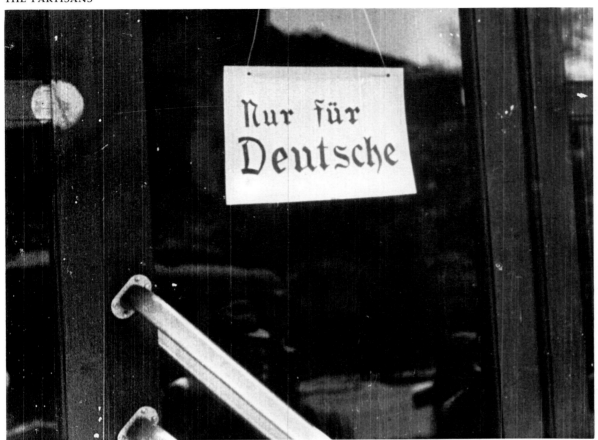

'For Germans only'. This was a familiar sign on shops, restaurants and public lavatories. Another similar sign read, 'Ukrainians and dogs not admitted'.

The main threat to the partisans always came from local people who collaborated with the enemy and informed on them. In this photograph, partisans have captured the starostas, the village chief appointed by the Germans who has been cooperating in the round-up and summary execution of Soviet deputies, Party and Komsomol members and their families. He will be tried by local people and partisans and, if found guilty, he will be shot or hanged.

In the occupied areas the police carried out executions of local people. This man, who has been working for the Germans as Chief of Police, has been taken prisoner by partisans. In some cases, as for example when the Red Army approached Orel, starostas, burgomasters, Russian policemen and other traitors were called up to redeem themselves and turn their weapons against the Germans by joining the partisans. Some did, but others retreated with their German masters.

After the liberation, a partisan is awarded a silver medal for bravery.

Kursk

After Stalingrad the Red Army seized the initiative and launched a massive offensive to oust the invaders. By April 1943 the Germans had been driven back some thousand kilometres (600–700 miles). In places they stood behind their lines of the previous summer. In response, the German High Command mustered all the forces it could for a summer campaign. It denuded its defences in Western Europe to send troops to the Eastern Front. By 1943 there were 198 divisions in Russia – more than at the time of the invasion. By shortening the front and by regrouping, with their new forces, the Germans managed to hold their ground temporarily. The Red Army took Kharkov, but after a stunning counter-offensive when the Russians had been forced to overstretch themselves, the enemy reoccupied it. Zhukov recaptured Voronezh, and further north Soviet forces had managed to create a salient 240 kilometres (150 miles) long and 160 kilometres (100 miles) wide, near the town of Kursk.

Even with reinforcements the German armies were incapable of advancing all along the line against the now immeasurably stronger Soviet Army. They planned an offensive called Operation Citadel – which concentrated 50 divisions on the flanks of the Soviet salient in order to exact revenge for the Stalingrad fiasco. By the end of June, 900,000 men, with 10,000 pieces of artillery, 2,700 tanks and 2,000 aircraft, were facing the Russians.

It was predictable that the Germans would decide to attack the Kursk salient. For the generals of the Third Reich, who had built their military success on the pincer movement, it was the natural place to attack. But the Stavka (the Moscow High Command) did not even have to rely on its foresight. It received detailed intelligence of the enemy plans through a stream of reports sent by a spy in the German High Command. They were also kept informed by the British tapping of the Enigma code machines as well as by other sources. A German prisoner gave the Red Army the precise time of the planned attack, the day before it was due to take place. This time, the Russians were ready.

The troops of the Central and Voronezh fronts – 1,300,000 men, up to 20,000 guns, 3,444 tanks and 2,172 planes – under the command of Generals Konstantin Rokossovsky and Nikolai Vatutin, were to absorb and repel the enemy attacks. Marshal Zhukov, the victor of Moscow and Stalingrad, was in overall command of the operation. His plan, known as 'Operation Kutuzov', was to allow the Germans to exhaust themselves and then to launch a massive counter-attack. To the rear, General Ivan Koniev's reserve Steppe Front waited with infantry, tank and motorized divisions to deliver the decisive blow. Since May, the Red Army had been at work laying mines and digging trenches. In some places these defences were 25 miles deep.

A Kursk veteran, belonging to a Guards regiment, armed with a 7.62mm PPSh 1941 sub-machine-gun. By the end of the war large numbers of soldiers wore moustaches, partly to save razor blades, but also as a gesture of machismo. Beards, however, remained a rarity, except among very old soldiers.

The battle of Kursk.

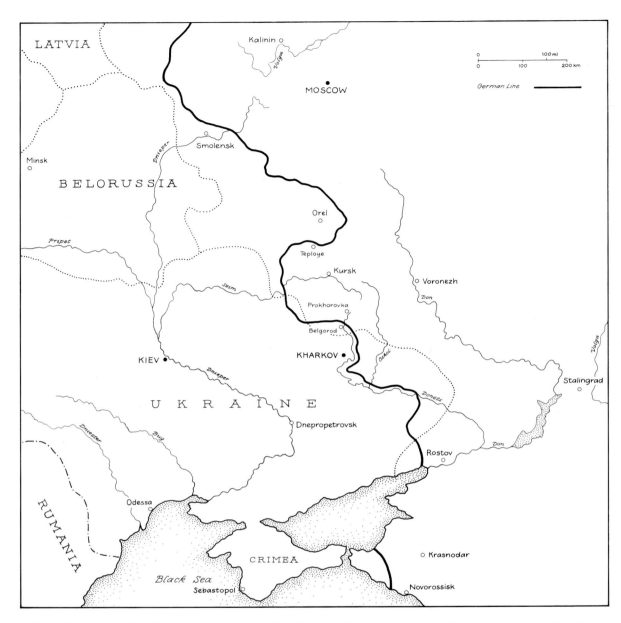

The German offensive began, as the Russians had known it would, at sunrise on 5th July. Heavy air preparation was followed by the southward attack by the Ninth Army on a 35-mile front. General Ehrfurt of the German Army Staff later recalled: '. . . the entire offensive force that the German Army could muster was hurled into action to expedite Operation Citadel.'

After two days the Germans had only penetrated seven miles into the salient. Then they began to surge ahead in the south. By 9th July they had covered twenty miles, at the most, in the south and twelve miles in the north. Some units had hardly moved since the end of the first day's fighting. Heavy rains, which had turned the wheat-fields around Kursk into a swamp, helped to slow the enemy advance.

The first Soviet communiqué stated that 'our troops have crippled or destroyed 586 enemy tanks . . . 203 enemy planes have been shot down.' A Western correspondent noted that 'it was the 586 tanks which captured the country's imagination: there had never been anything like it in one day. The feeling it produced was like that in London at the height of the Battle of Britain.'

The Germans had behaved exactly as Zhukov had predicted. The more fuel and ammunition they could be encouraged to use up in the first few days of the fighting, the easier it would be for him to defeat them, when he chose to do so.

The 12th July was a hot day on the steppe. The ground that had so recently been marshy had dried out. The Germans had decided to launch attempts to break through the Russian lines simultaneously in the north of the salient, near Teploye, and to the south, near Prokhorovka. Colonel-General Hoth, in the south, had mustered 600 tanks. But he had to contend with 850 Soviet tanks, manned by fresh, confident crews. Hoth and the Russian commander, Lt-General Rotmistrov, had clashed violently once before, at Stalingrad, when the Germans had tried unsuccessfully to break through to relieve their surrounded forces.

The two armies met on a narrow strip of land between the Psel River and a railway embankment. The area was covered with little hills, orchards, ravines and gullies. Hidden among the cornfields lay Soviet anti-tank batteries and landmines. The earth shook for eight hours as the two forces engaged in the fiercest tank fighting in history. The Luftwaffe and the Red Air Force intended to support their respective forces from the air, but the fighting was so close that it was impossible for them to do so without risking their own tanks. The planes could only attack each other, in a series of dog-fights that went on throughout the day. On the ground, tank crews collided, unable to find their way through the dust clouds, smoke, burning tanks and exploding landmines. By nightfall the Germans had made no headway at all.

The German assault near Teploye in the north of the Kursk salient had been pre-empted by a Soviet counter-offensive. Aware that the Germans were committing most of their strength to the assault against Kursk, the Russians attacked the Orel salient to the north of the Kursk bulge. The attack was undertaken by elements of the Briansk Front, commanded by General Popov, and the Western Front under General Sokolovsky, and it proved so successful that the Germans were forced to withdraw four committed and reserve divisions from the Ninth Army.

British and American forces had already landed in Sicily, and Italy appeared to be at the point of collapse. At last the Allies were beginning to relieve the pressure on the Soviet Union. Hitler was forced to withdraw troops from Russia to reinforce the Axis power in the Mediterranean, and to call a halt to Operation Citadel.

On 5th August, Yuri Levitan made an announcement of a sort that was to become pleasantly familiar during the next two years: 'Today, 5th August, the troops of the Briansk Front, in co-operation with the troops of the Western and Central Fronts, captured, as a result of bitter fighting, the City of Orel. Today also the troops of the Steppe and Voronezh Fronts broke the enemy's resistance and captured the town of Belgorod.'

The German tank crews who had fought so successfully in the Western campaigns were eager in July 1943 for revenge after their defeat at Stalingrad.

At Kursk the Russians greatly outnumbered the Germans in men and guns. Numbers of armoured vehicles and aircraft were roughly equal.

	Germany	Russia
Men	900,000	1,337,000
Guns	10,000	20,220
Vehicles	2,700	3,306
Aircraft	2,500	2,650

A Zis-11 57mm anti-tank gun engages a German tank (on the horizon). These guns were so powerful that their shells could penetrate 140 mm of armour at a range of 50 metres (160 ft). In 1942, production of the Zis-11 was stopped, on the basis that lighter guns could destroy tanks just as well. But a year later, when the Germans developed the Tiger tank, the Zis-11 came into its own again, because it was thought to be the only gun that could attack it effectively.

Soviet artillery began bombarding the enemy positions 30 minutes before the Germans had planned to attack. At this stage all their troops were concentrated in the assembly positions. German losses were so heavy in this pre-emptive strike that they had to delay their attack. In this photograph, taken during the bombardment, a wounded Russian soldier stumbles towards his gun – a 152mm field Howitzer, model 1943 (D–1), which had a range of 12,400 metres (13,565 yds) and fired a high explosive shell weighing 51.1 kilograms (112.6 lb).

Facing page: In the forward trenches on the eve of the offensive, Marshal Konstantin Rokossovsky checks the plans for dealing with the German attack, details of which had been known to Russian Intelligence since April. He is surrounded by field telephones and signal equipment, which were critically important during the battle. Rokossovsky is wearing the Order of Suvorov, which he was awarded after Stalingrad. This is a very high order, given only during wartime, for defeating the enemy when heavily outnumbered in a major operation.

On the black, scorched earth the gutted tanks burnt like torches. It was difficult to establish which side was attacking and which defending. The 2nd Battalion 181st Tank Brigade of XVIII Tank Corps, attacking on the left bank of the Psel, encountered a group of Tigers which opened fire on the Soviet armoured fighting vehicles from a stationary position. The powerful long-range guns of the Tigers are exceedingly dangerous, and the Soviet tanks had to try to close with them as quickly as possible to eliminate this advantage of the enemy. Captain P. A. Skripkin, the battalion commander, ordered: 'Forward, follow me!' The first shell of the commander's tank pierced the side of a Tiger. Instantly another Tiger opened fire on Skripkin's T-34. A shell crashed through its side and a second wounded the battalion commander. The driver and wireless operator pulled their commander from the tank and took him to the cover of a shell crater. As a Tiger was making straight for them, Aleksandr Nikolayev, the driver, leapt back into his damaged and already smouldering tank, started the engine and raced up to meet the enemy tank. Like a flaming ball of fire the T-34 raced over the ground. The Tiger halted. But it was too late. The blazing tank rammed the German Panzer at full speed. The detonation made the ground shake.

This Tiger tank and the crew member have both been badly burnt; the Tiger was put out of action by a direct hit from a shell under the turret.

By mid-1942 the Germans had four main designs of tank: heavy (Tiger); medium (Panther); Pz III and Pz IV. On the Soviet side, almost all tank production consisted of two types only: the T34 and the KV, but the numbers manufactured far exceeded German tank production.

Facing page: A badly wounded Red Army soldier exhorts his comrades to the attack.

During the battle. A T34 tank loaded with infantry passes a 76.2mm field gun, model 1942 SIS3 (76–42).

'There is a specific point about the performance of an anti-tank gun which we learned from personal experience. Once it engages tanks it cannot quit, it can only win or perish. A foot soldier or a tank may withdraw from action at practically any stage. But not the anti-tank gun.

When the first enemy tanks appeared, we all started counting them. I personally tried several times but lost count. I began again and gave up. I remember the last time I got to something like 30. But more and more came lumbering out of the wood . . . were there 36 of them, or more or less? . . . it no longer made much difference to us.

Only when the distance between us and the tanks was 450 to 500 metres did we open fire. One after another the tanks went out of commission.

The enemy, apparently, never dreamed that one gun dared to engage 36 tanks and an infantry landing. No doubt they thought they had run into considerable forces. When the tanks started going out of commission they must have been confirmed in that belief.'

Captain Nikolai Kanischev – excerpt from his diary.

The Red Army built a wide network of trenches and passes which gave the troops a mobile and flexible defence system. The trenches were built in rows, with passes connecting them so that the soldiers could retreat if necessary. Each pass was guarded by a machine-gun nest.

The Russians decided to allow the Germans to attack at Kursk, so that they could knock out as many tanks as possible before counter-attacking.

Here, a Maxim 1910 76.2mm machine gun, on a Sokolov mounting, supports a Soviet infantry company on the edge of the Kursk Salient in June 1943.

When a tank came at me the first time, I was sure that that was the end of the world, honest to God. Then that tank came nearer and started burning and I thought to myself – it's the end for him, not me. You know, by the way, I rolled and smoked about 5 cigarettes during that battle. Well, perhaps not right to the end, I don't want to lie to you, but I did roll 5 cigarettes. When you're in combat it's this way: you put your gun aside and light a cigarette, when time allows. You can smoke when a battle's on, what you can't do is miss your aim. If you miss, you won't need that cig. That's the way it is.

A soldier takes the oath.

Facing page: *Pilots swearing their oath before the regimental banner. The oath began: 'I, a citizen of the Union of Soviet Socialist Republics, vow, while I am in the ranks of the Armed Forces, this oath, and solemnly swear to be an honourable, brave, disciplined and vigilant soldier, to guard the military secrets strictly, and to execute without any contradiction, all military regulations and the order of my commanders and superiors.' It continues to include vows to learn the skills of warfare and above all else to defend until death the Soviet homeland. It concludes, 'Should I break my solemn oath, may the severe punishment of Soviet law and the universal hatred and contempt of the labouring masses strike me.'*

One of the toughest jobs during the war was moving the heavy guns, together with ammunition boxes and shells, over rough terrain. Each gun crew was responsible for pulling its own weapon. Some days during the battle of Kursk, Russian gun crews advanced as much as 20 kilometres (12½ miles). Often they had to advance and retreat several times in a day, pausing to fire at German tanks. The gun shown is the 76.2mm field gun, model 1942 SIS3 (76–42), which had a travelling weight of 1,120 kilograms (2,470 lb). Each of its shells weighed 6.21 kilograms (13.7 lb).

. . . The men did not sleep on the eve of a battle, and did all kinds of chores. They were in that tranquil frame of mind that people usually experience before a major event in their lives. They mended their clothing, made their boots fit so their feet would be comfortable, examined their weapons and shaved one another. One of the soldiers wanted to change into new underwear, but the others stopped him, saying: 'What's the matter, you getting set to die?! Wait a while, there's still a lot of fighting ahead. Plenty of time for that.' The oldtimers said to him, 'Keep that underwear till victory day. You'll need it when you go home.'

Experienced flying officers in the forward trenches often directed bombers to their targets by radio. Here a major in the Air Force maintains radio communication with controllers on the ground.

The Ilyushin 11–2 Shturmovik, probably the most famous of all Russian planes during World War II. Some 36,163 planes were produced between 1941 and 1944. It was known as the 'flying tank' because of its heavy armour which machine-gun fire could not penetrate. It could fly very low and was, therefore, very difficult to shoot down. Its only weak spot was the cabin of the radio operator, who was also the gunner. The plane itself and the pilot usually survived an attack, but losses of gunners were heavy.

Anti-tank bombs were used for the first time during the battle of Kursk. They would penetrate the tank and explode inside.

A PO2 light bomber ground support aircraft.

Russian troops counter-attack. The T34 tanks in this photograph are all armed with the older style 76mm gun. Infantrymen rode into battle on the sides of the tanks, but when the enemy fire became intense it was safer for them to run alongside.

A field of wheat on fire during the battle of Kursk.

A German soldier whose gun has been put out of action awaits capture by the Russians. The Russians put the German losses at Kursk at 70,000 killed, 2,000 tanks destroyed and 195 mobile guns, 844 field guns, 5,000 motor vehicles captured, and 1,392 planes destroyed.

Signal flares illuminate the terrain for night attacks.

The Russian flag was hoisted over Orel on 5th August 1943. That same day, over Moscow Radio, came Stalin's order of the day: 'Tonight at twenty-four o'clock, on 5th August, the capital of our country, Moscow, will salute the valiant troops that liberated Orel and Belgorod with twelve artillery salvoes from 120 guns. I express my thanks to all the troops that took part in the offensive . . . Eternal glory to the heroes who fell in the struggle for the freedom of our country. Death to the German invaders.'

Two provincial capitals were liberated as a result of the battle of Kursk – Belgorod and Orel. Of Orel's pre-1941 population of 114,000 only 30,000 survived. It was said that 12,000 were murdered by the Germans and 24,000 were deported as slave labourers to the Reich. The winter of 1941–2 had been the hardest, during which hundreds had died of starvation. Half the city was totally destroyed and all its bridges blown when the Red Army liberated it on 5th August 1943.

At the beginning of the war there was still some complacency. 'We are sure to win' was the general belief and this confidence had a certain negative effect. For since victory would be ours, since we would win anyway, perhaps there was no need for a superhuman effort on our part, perhaps things would work out without us. But the Germans poured on the lead without looking. A bitter joke in circulation from Stalingrad times told of a soldier going into battle carrying 150 cartridges; when he was carried to the field hospital, he had 151 – he hadn't even had a chance to fire his gun.

There was another extreme – contempt of death. This was written about and acclaimed as valour. But by mid-1942 there was too much of this contempt around, and yet the distance to victory was as great as ever . . . Sometimes the going gets so hard that death seems a welcome deliverance. Those are no empty words. Gradually they stopped writing about this contempt of death. The mission of the soldier was not to die with dashing defiance, but to kill the enemy.

The Liberation of the Country

With the Battle of Kursk the Soviet Armed Forces were able to seize the strategic initiative. The Wehrmacht were limited to defensive operations. The Red Army started to free the territories the invaders had seized in 1941–2. The liberation was carried out in ten separate offensives launched at various points along a 2,000-mile front. In the autumn of 1943 the Germans had fallen back to the west side of the River Dnieper. Kharkov fell to the Red Army on 23rd August, Smolensk on 25th September and Kiev on 6th November.

On 14th January 1944 the first of the ten offensives, usually known as the Liberation of Leningrad, began. Between 14th and 27th January 1944 Soviet forces smashed through the German defensive positions around the city. The Red Army cleared the territory southwards as far as Novgorod, and then during the next fortnight pushed its way westwards to take Luga, about 80 miles south of Leningrad. Very heavy artillery concentrations were used in this offensive – 500,000 shells were fired at the German fortifications on the first day of the offensive alone. Such artillery attacks had become standard Soviet practice. German casualties were high, and so were their losses of tanks and guns. The main purpose of this offensive, to free the Moscow–Leningrad railway, was achieved on 27th January.

The second offensive, in the Ukraine, took place in February and March in such difficult conditions that it became known as 'the mud offensive'. Four Red Army Fronts were involved, in a series of violent attacks that ejected the Germans from the southern and eastern parts of the Ukraine. Once again German losses, both in men and equipment, were extremely heavy.

The third offensive took Odessa, the Black Sea port, and liberated the Crimea. Outflanked from the north, Odessa fell on 10th April 1944, and then the Red Army directed its attention to the Crimea, which Hitler stubbornly insisted should be held at all costs. Fighting continued throughout April, and Sebastopol eventually fell on 19th May 1944, bringing the north shore of the Black Sea under Soviet control once again.

The fourth offensive was against Finland. Taking advantage of the German invasion of Russia, Finland had joined in the attack, hoping to retrieve the territory ceded under the Treaty of Moscow on 12th March 1940. Finnish troops had moved beyond their 1939 border frontier, although it must be said that most Finns were decidedly antipathetic towards their German 'ally'. Tentative peace talks had taken place in neutral Sweden, but the Soviet government felt that only armed force would bring the Finns to the negotiating table. Accordingly the offensive began on 9th June 1944 and was directed along the Karelian isthmus through to Viborg. Within two days the Finnish–German defences had been broken and by the end of July the Finns had been pushed back to the 1940 frontier. The Red Army stopped there, without pursuing its advance to the Finnish capital.

Until 1936, all Soviet mortar equipment had been of French or German origin, obtained either during World War I, or during the period of Soviet-German military co-operation, following the Treaty of Rapallo in the 1920s. In 1936, however, the Russians introduced the first of their indigenous types, the 82mm mortar, M 1936. Soviet mortars ranged from a 50mm calibre to that of 160mm.

The fifth offensive took place in Belorussia in June and July. The attack was launched on 23rd June, with Soviet forces moving north of the Pripet marshes and crossing into Poland on a wide front. By the beginning of August, Soviet troops were crossing the river Nieman. On 1st August 1944 the Polish Home Army began its uprising against the Germans. Logistic difficulties prevented Soviet troops from assisting them to any extent. For 63 days the Poles battled with the Germans and their eastern European auxiliaries, who carried out acts of unbelievable atrocity against the civilian population. When the Polish commander surrendered on 3rd October 1944 Warsaw was devastated, with over 200,000 of its citizens dead.

The sixth offensive cleared the Western Ukraine, and took place in July and August. The Red Army liberated Lwow and forced the Vistula, and after an abortive attempt to break through to Cracow, established the important bridgehead of Sandomierz on the west bank of the River Vistula, south of Warsaw. But after its failure to take Warsaw, the Red Army did not pursue its objective of breaking through to Germany at any price. Here in Poland the concentration of German forces was heavier than anywhere else.

The seventh offensive in August cut deep into Germany's ally Rumania. After trapping fifteen German and several Rumanian divisions in the Jassy-Kishenev 'pockets' the Red Army swept into Rumania proper. A *coup d'état* on 23rd August removed the pro-Axis dictator Marshal Ion Antonescu, and Rumania now joined the fight against its former ally. The Red Army entered Bucharest on 31st August and then went on to over-run Bulgaria and eastern Yugoslavia, in contact with Tito's units, to reach the borders of Hungary.

The eighth offensive cleared the Baltic states of Estonia and most of Latvia in September and October. On 29th September Tallin, the seaport capital of Estonia, fell to the Soviet forces while another thrust turned south-westwards to make for the Latvian capital Riga, which was

Welcoming the Soviet army.

German Line 1 December 1943 ....
German Line 23 June 1944 ————
German Line 15 December 1944 — — —
German Line 7 May 1945 —·—·—·

liberated on 23rd October. Thirty German divisions remained in the Courland Peninsula, constituting a 'nuisance' force until the eventual capitulation of Germany.

The ninth offensive lasted from October until December. Its main objective was to defeat the Axis forces in Hungary, the last remaining German ally in Europe. The Red Army entered Yugoslavia on 23rd September. Within a month the Russians, together with Marshal Tito's Yugoslav partisans, had liberated most of the country, including the capital. Red Army forces, accompanied by Rumanian and Bulgarian units, then pressed on into Hungary, where German–Hungarian divisions were holding out in the capital, Budapest. Fighting raged around the city for two months, but without success, so the Russian forces bypassed it. By the end of December most of Hungary had been liberated and Red Army troops reached Czechoslovakia.

The tenth offensive took place in October, in the far north, in Lapland. The Red Army's objective was to take the port of Petsamo and other points from which the Allied convoys bringing vital war material to Murmansk could be protected. After the usual heavy artillery bombardment of the German positions, Soviet troops broke through the defences and within three days took Petsamo. A week later, the Red Army had cleared the surrounding area and had moved into northern Norway, the Finnmark Province.

These successes were not won easily. It is estimated that 1,400,000 men died during the liberation offensives.

Liberation: the Russian winter offensive of 1944.

181

Soviet soldiers engaged in a street fight at Sebastopol. The city was liberated on 9th May 1944. The British foreign correspondent, Alexander Werth, observed that the Russians had defended the city for 250 days in 1941 and 1942, in spite of being heavily outnumbered by the Germans. In 1944 the two sides were roughly equal in strength and it took only four days to eject the Nazis. The Germans had not suffered from any shortages because they were receiving supplies through the Black Sea ports.

This woman was among the few inhabitants of Sebastopol not to have been evacuated.

PO–2 night bombers returning to their base at dawn. These planes were known as 'coffee-grinders' because of the incessant noise they made. This was not the only disadvantage of the PO–2. The cabin was completely open to the air, except for a windshield.

PE–2 bombers. It was difficult for enemy fighters to approach these planes when they were flying in formation, because of the high density of fire they could produce.

The PE–2, designed by Vladimir Mikhailovich Petlyakov who died in a flying accident in January 1942, equipped the majority of Soviet bomber regiments during World War II. It had a range of 1,000–1,500 kilometres (621–931 miles) and carried twelve 100-kilogram bombs.

PE–2 bombers during a bombing raid. These twin-engined planes were used for hitting troop concentrations, airfields, railway stations, bridges and so on. In the second half of 1943 the design was modified so that the plane could dive-bomb. Having put the aircraft into a dive the pilot aimed at a target, dropped the bombs and pulled the aircraft out of the dive, causing great stress both to the aircraft and to the pilot.

Yak–7 fighters in action over Belorussia, with a German bomber spinning out of sight.

At the beginning of the war the Red Air Force planes were seriously outdated, and most of the modern planes it possessed were destroyed on the ground in the first hours of the war. But by the end of 1942, Soviet industry was producing modern planes in large numbers, continually improving their design.

Yak fighters were very light, and they could operate from dirt airfields – a great advantage in Russia at the time. They were equipped with powerful armaments, and had a high rate of fire. They did not, however, have a very broad radius of action because they could not carry much fuel.

In all, some 6,399 Yak–7s were built. After the IL–11 assault planes, they were the most common plane produced in the Soviet Union during the war. They were used for rocket boost experiments, which continued until the first Soviet jet-propelled aircraft, the Yak–15, made its test flight on 24th April 1946.

Infantrymen moving in on a small village in which German troops are still holed up. German prisoners taken in the Ukraine, while bitterly disappointed at having been caught, still showed much fighting spirit, believing in the Führer's promised miracle weapon of Vergeltung (revenge).

Facing page: *By the Dnieper, 1944.*

Members of a small commando unit fighting to recapture a Ukrainian village. The Germans regarded the Ukraine as an important source of food. Attempts to win over the local population were thwarted by the oppressive régime of Reichskommissar Erich Koch, who referred to the Ukrainians as 'niggers'.

Hidden from the enemy by low hills, we make our way through a ravine to the approach trenches. It's dank and foggy, but we warm up as we walk. The enemy is a stone's throw from us. In places, our entrenchments are only a few dozen metres away from the Germans, in other places a trench is separated by obstacles and wooden pickets. We're on this side and the Germans are on the other. The snipers' nests are dug between the battle outposts and the firing line. The enemy's defences are visible from here.

German speech is heard in the trenches and the foreign faces can sometimes be distinguished with the naked eye. Some of the men on both sides of the firing line have come to know each other by sight. The appearance of an officer in the enemy trench is heralded by the clicking of heels and a barked command. That's when the fun begins.

The men fling hand-grenades and the Nazis reciprocate with grenades on long wooden handles. Our boys have become expert in catching them in mid-air and tossing them back.

Liudmilla Pavlichenko, a sniper who killed more than 300 Germans.

'I joined the army at a time when women were not yet accepted there, especially women snipers. I had the option of becoming a nurse. But I refused because I had learned to shoot before the war. Only after my insistent requests did the regimental commander take me on as a sniper.

I did not take up arms because I wanted to kill, but because I had seen ruined cities, villages razed to the ground, bereaved children, old folk, women and infants murdered . . .'

The Dnieper river crossing is what I'm not likely to forget for as long as I live. We were all to contrive our own landing craft as best we could, so we made huge cushions by sewing armfuls of straw into our cloak-tents. Though I was born on the bank of the Amu Darya in Central Asia and was a good swimmer, I had an automatic rifle, two discs of ammunition, two grenades, a spade for digging in, a flask of water and a food ration I had to get across . . .

The night of 5th October 1943 was as dark as dark could be . . . We had got to the middle of the river when the German guns opened up on the right, high shore of the Dnieper. The water began to churn. I realized what a fish feels like when it's dynamited.

All I could think of was getting to the right bank quickly . . . that was where the shells couldn't reach me. The machine-gun fire seemed tame by comparison. I was more afraid of the drowning hands that kept catching at me on all sides.

After what seemed an eternity I felt solid ground underfoot. The beach was strewn with severed limbs and torn bodies. I'd thought the worst was behind us at Stalingrad and Kursk, but the Dnieper river crossing beat them in terms of savagery.

Reconnaissance units crossing the Kuban in the Crimea. The depth of the river varied dramatically here, so the men are using truck tyres as bathing rings, and plywood oars to paddle.

Soldiers at the front
receive a bundle of mail
from home. Envelopes
were very hard to come
by during the war, so
people folded their letters
up instead. Service
personnel folded their
letters into triangles, and
these were carried free of
charge.

Sebastopol. The crew of a large-calibre Navy gun relaxing in their armoured gun shelter.

Producing a divisional newspaper at the front. The type was all set manually, on a portable plant that moved around with the troops. Each front, each army and each division produced its own newspaper. The national newspapers were also distributed to the Army – Pravda, Izvestia, Komsomol *and* Trut. *There was also the* Red Star *newspaper, produced daily by the People's Commissariat for Defence (the equivalent of the Ministry of Defence). A quarter-sheet Divisional leaflet was produced every day, or when necessary.*

The larger military units set up their own tailors' shops, staffed by soldiers who had been tailors in peacetime. These shops repaired uniforms, and altered them to fit when necessary. Following Russian successes in 1942 and 1943 uniforms were smartened up.

With their tank camouflaged by netting, members of a tank crew clean themselves up. There were never enough experienced barbers in the army, so most soldiers just cut each other's hair and helped each other to shave when there were no mirrors. The man who is being shaved is wearing the Orders of the Red Star and the Patriotic War, the former created in 1930, the latter in 1942.

After a period at the front, a unit would withdraw for rest and relaxation. This included tidying up their uniforms. Here, a group of young soldiers are sewing clean collars into their jackets. Their heads have probably been shaved for sanitary reasons — front-line troops sometimes couldn't shower for months. The soldier in the foreground is wearing puttees rather than jackboots; puttees were not usually worn as they tended to hamper circulation.

A 'Russian' (Turkish) bath was one of the greatest treats imaginable for a weary and grimy soldier. Troops often built bath-houses for themselves or adapted existing buildings for the purpose.

Soldiers in the Red Army were allowed 100 grams of vodka after a visit to the 'Russian' baths or after heavy fighting. There was a tradition in the army of 'rinsing the order' – a newly awarded medal or badge of rank would be dropped into a glass of vodka. The soldier would drink the vodka and then, without using his hands, take hold of the order between his teeth.

Enterprising airmen, dissatisfied with their allocation of vodka, discovered a method of extracting alcohol from the shock-absorbers in their planes. They poured the liquid through their gas masks, filtering out the impurities, so that they were left with more or less neat alcohol. They added syrup to this, and drank the 'chassis liqueur' with pleasure.

Soldiers and nurses dancing in a sunlit forest glade.

No one had an easy time of it at the front. That was especially true for us girls.

From the outset girls enlisted even when they had to forge their birth dates from age 17 to 19. But soon we were being called up, too.

Most of us thought the war was something heroically romantic and the very first brush with reality had a sobering effect.

Yes, it was difficult everywhere. The badly wounded were so helpless they had to be cared for. The wards were crowded, the air was heavy with scents that were anything but perfume. The younger men who were recovering courted the nurses insistently. There was no threatening them with the front line – that was where they were all headed anyway. What was a girl to say to a soldier who was going to battle tomorrow, whose chance of returning was very slim and who, on top of everything else, was so attractive – see you after the war?

It is easy to talk about it today. At that time, death stood ready and waiting behind each and every one of us. Besides, life will go its own way, even if there's a war on. Marriages were solemnized. Regimental orders pronounced couples man and wife and changed the wife's name to her husband's. Abortions, banned in the country in those days, were permitted at field hospitals. Those who wished to have their babies were demobbed, provided with an allowance and sent home. Many of us remained single all our lives. The happiness of front-line love was short-lived.

Facing page: *A woman soldier kneeling near a 122mm field Howitzer, model 1938, ironing her uniform. The iron was heated by being filled with hot charcoal.*

Soldiers in the Ukraine washing clothes. Large army units had laundries, but it was not uncommon for the men to have to cope with washing their own clothes.

A boy soldier wearing the Order of Glory, an award instituted in 1943 and given to rank and file soldiers for extraordinary valour. He was probably attached to a reconnaissance unit.

Facing page: A Soviet mortar crew asleep after fighting all night. The Red Army laid great emphasis on the use of mortars; in an offensive role they were usually employed en masse to devastating effect.

One of the most popular songs at the end of the war was The Nightingale, written in the front lines late in 1944:

'Sing softly,
   nightingales,
   nightingales,
Let the soldiers have
   some sleep. . . .
Spring is here in the
   front lines
And the boys have lost
   all peace,
But not because the
   guns are
   booming. . . .
The nightingales give
   them no rest,
They're back again and
   with no thought
For the fighting all
   around
The madcap
   nightingales
Are singing once
   again.'

Lyrics: Alexei Fatyanov; music: Vasilii Solovyov-Sedoi.

Dogs and cats whose owners had been killed often attached themselves to army units.

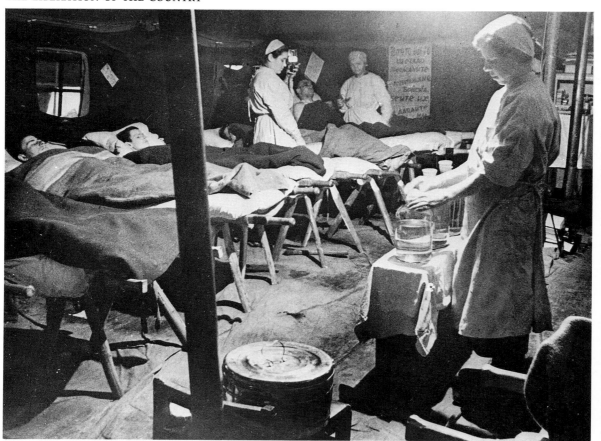

A nurse sterilizes bandages at a field hospital. The wounded were taken as soon as possible to tent hospitals like this one. Those who could be moved would then be transferred to hospitals in the rear. The rest would remain, on makeshift beds that were just stretchers on wooden stands.

A woman, from a liberated village, is prepared for burial. According to old Russian superstition, the lid of the coffin must never be brought into the house, and a woman's head must be covered for burial.

There was a shortage of coffins during the war, so many people, especially servicemen, were buried wrapped in overcoats.

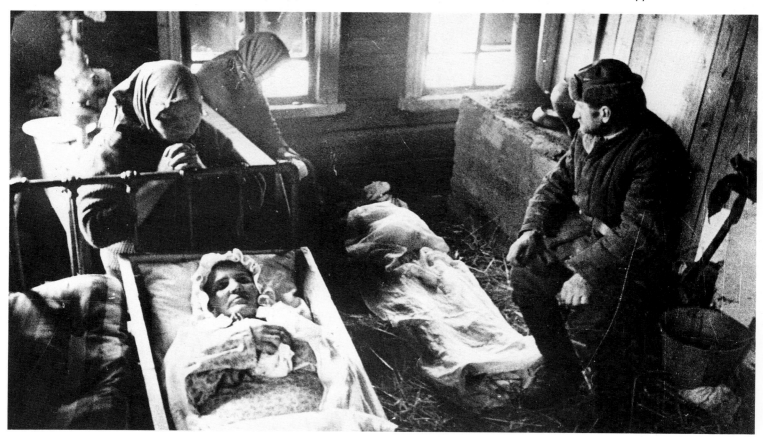

Soldiers eating American tinned pork, supplied under the Lend-Lease Agreement, in a dug-out. Between 1942 and 1945 the USA sent 4 million tons of general supplies to Russia. Russian troops called them the 'second front', an ironic reference to the lack of a Western Front between 1941 and 1944.

On cold nights I shared a greatcoat with quite a few of my wartime comrades in the fighting lines. Many of them have since fallen . . . There is no brotherhood that binds people closer than the brotherhood that's born in the lines, and a shared greatcoat is one of its symbols. You feel warm and secure with a friend close by.

Actually, there are two greatcoats for two. A shared greatcoat is just a figure of speech. So what happens to the second?

Duffel bags or lambskin mittens (with two fingers so it's easier to shoot) are used for pillows. The individual tents that double up as cloaks are used as mattresses and the greatcoats are the blankets. The shabbier one covers the feet and legs and the newer one the upper part of the bodies. Both men settle down on the same side. If there is the blessed chance of taking off your boots, the feet are tucked into the sleeves of the greatcoat – a pair of feet to a sleeve. The upper greatcoat is pulled over the shoulders, the shoulder of one fits into the right sleeve, the shoulder of the other into the left. The result is a kind of sleeping bag, warm and cosy. If it gets inordinately cold, the greatcoat is pulled over the heads – one head in one sleeve, the other in the other.

When one side goes numb and the other freezes stiff, both men turn over simultaneously and the fitful sleep of the soldiers continues . . .

At Poti, on the Black
Sea, torpedoes are loaded
onto a submarine. The
main Soviet Naval bases
in the Black Sea were
first Sebastopol, then
Novorossirsk, then
Tuapse and finally Poti,
near the Turkish border.
The ship in the
background is the pre-
Revolutionary cruiser
Krasny Krim.

Torpedo boats, built out of plywood and equipped with aircraft engines (making them very light and very fast) patrol the Black Sea. They were used against German transport ships. If one of these torpedo boats took a direct hit, almost nothing of it survived. The strength of the Soviet Navy during World War II lay more in small vessels like these than in larger units, such as battleships or cruisers.

A depth charge is dropped from a Sea Hunter onto an enemy submarine. Sea Hunters were used to seek out and destroy German submarines, and to escort other ships.

The Germans built such powerful defence lines in the Karpaty mountains that it was impossible to storm them with a frontal attack. The Russians had to attack them from the flanks. This entailed hauling guns and ammunition along with them, over the mountains. This box of artillery shells must have weighed at least 50 kg.

Soviet soldiers heading for the front, in the Caucasus mountains. It was vital to prevent the Germans from reaching Baku and gaining control of the last remaining naval bases. Glaciers in the Caucasus mountains still carry weapons and dead bodies, perfectly preserved in ice, that date from the war.

The foot soldier packs a load that could rival a mule's. Those who are on the short side cannot be seen for all the gear. There's the rolled greatcoat over the shoulder, the duffel bag, the gas mask (drat it), the helmet and the sapper's spade, the flask and mess tin, and the field bag or map case . . .

Sometimes you stuff an anti-tank grenade into the gas-mask bag and there's another bag for cartridges and there's the ammo. That's not counting the weapons – a rifle or sub-machine-gun and pistol. And that getup, mind you, is not for walking on and off stage . . .

When it's hot, the sweat comes pouring down. The cliché should be taken literally in our case. Eyes are blurred with salt tears, sweat trickles under the collar, darkens the shoulders . . . As for the boots – you could wash spoons in them. It isn't every day that you come across water. It's not every day the soldier can wash his togs. Greyish salt blotches the field blouse when it dries in the sun. Take it off and it can stand stiff.

The Russian spring is traditionally the time of rasputitsa, *the season of bad roads. Many of the roads outside the big cities turn to mud. The mud in the spring of 1944 was worse than usual. Here, six horses are pulling a gun along a virtually impassable track.*

In the Ukraine, spring 1944: soldiers try to manoeuvre a truck loaded with artillery shells that is stuck in the mud.

It would take no ordinary imagination to picture the dust of the frontline roads. Till practically the end of the war the infantry advanced along unpaved roads that had been pulverized to what seemed the very heart of the earth. Boots sank ankle-deep into dust. Puttees were covered with a solid grey film.

When the order for a brief halt was given, the soldiers collapsed into the dust. Some fell right in a wayside ditch without bothering to put their duffel bags under their heads, just so they could put their feet up higher. We learned to lie jack-knifed side by side, with heads well above the dust on each other's thighs.

Vehicles, artillery and sometimes tanks would overtake the marching columns, and raise a wall of dust that impeded our breathing. The dust gritted on our teeth and penetrated everywhere. Only the teeth and eyeballs showed white. When eyelids dropped a coat of dust fluttered off the eyelashes.

The Red Army mostly travelled on foot. Behind the infantryman a 37mm anti-tank gun is being brought into position.

A radio operator, using a portable, shortwave radio, contacts a reconnaissance group behind enemy lines.

The Katyusha rocket launcher was used for the first time in 1941 near the town of Orsha in Belorussia. Its screaming sound was to become familiar to German soldiers during the next few years. Each launcher truck could fire sixteen rockets simultaneously, and although the elevation of the rockets was variable, aiming them simply meant pointing the truck in the right direction. The Katyusha had a range of 9,000 metres and took about ten minutes to reload. The Germans called them 'Stalin Organs'.

The Germans were convinced that their defences on the right bank of the Dnieper were impenetrable. But Soviet troops managed to cross the river in several places and establish bridgeheads. Over 3,000 men were awarded the title 'Hero of the Soviet Union' after this operation, out of a total of 11,000 such awards in the entire war.

Here, soldiers are building a pontoon bridge across the Dnieper, while keeping watch for enemy planes. The sign on the left of the photograph says 'Forward to Kiev'.

How to carry a gun across a river without getting your uniform wet.

The people in the liberated villages have nothing to offer us, no refreshment. The enemy has destroyed everything.

The women eat sunflower seeds. The Germans arrogantly call them 'Russian chocolate'. But we don't mind, we enjoy them. They help make the time go by faster on the march. I'm not used to these seeds so I take my time about them. They've turned into a kind of speedometer for me. When I've finished a pocketful, I know we've covered 10 kilometres. I don't have to count.

Soldiers rolling their own cigarettes, using the cheap Makhorka tobacco. Rolling papers were difficult to find so the men used any sort of paper they could – usually sheets of the regimental newspaper. Even before the war no Western-style cigarettes were produced in the Soviet Union. There were only Papierossi, paper pipes half full of tobacco. These were very hard to come by during the war, and it was usually only the senior officers who managed to lay their hands on them. Stalin himself favoured a Dunhill pipe.

An informal troop concert. Apart from Katyusha, *other popular songs among Russian troops included* Little Blue Scarf, Into the Battle for the Country, Into Battle for Stalin, Sacred War, The Dark Night *and* Kostyn, The Odessa Sailor.

During the advance, the boys from Company One found an old-fashioned phonograph with a horn in a village that had been set on fire by German torchbearers. The soldiers lugged it along wherever the fighting took them, and treasured the few records they had. One of those records was *Stenka Razin*. The Nazis often heard us playing it in the night and even tried to get us to play it again and again.

'Ivan,' they'd shout, 'play Volga, Volga.'

The reply was: 'You want the Volga, eh? Well, you're not getting it. Ever!'

We are travelling along a cart-track in territory recently cleared of the Germans. There are signs of heavy fighting everywhere. The earth is pockmarked with holes made by shells, mines and bombs. As we move forward we come across more and more corpses of men and horses. The sweetly nauseating smell of death impels us to hold our breath . . .

We enter what was but recently a village. Ruins of razed homes . . . soot-covered smokestacks on all sides . . . Leaving our vehicle we follow a little old woman silently down what was once a street. Two hens run wild. Seeing men in khaki they fling themselves out of the way without their usual cackling and disappear.

'Stupid birds', the old lady said. 'They think you are Germans.' She then told us that in captured villages the Germans hunted down ducks, geese and chickens.

The men are all away fighting, the women and children have taken cover in the nearby forests. Now they return to their razed village and roam about the ruins in the hope of finding at least something that has remained.

In 1942, Air Force major Seryogin was rescued by the Ossachuk family, having been shot down in the occupied Ukraine. Mrs Ossachuk, a schoolteacher, hid him from the Germans, nursed him back to health and helped him to return to his unit.

In August 1943, when the Ossachuks' village was liberated, Seryogin visited them, bringing a bottle of Soviet champagne and food for a feast. Flyers and submarine crews had access to better food than anyone else during the war, an acknowledgement of their expertise and the relative danger of the work they had to do.

The battle is still raging. On the far end of the village the enemy is still massing for a counter-attack to drive us out of the village . . . when, from out of the cellars and basements of half-ruined houses, out of dugouts, running, climbing and clambering, come our long-suffering countrymen – miraculous survivors.

Dressed in indescribable rags, in clothes gone threadbare over the years of occupation, bundled up, muffled in shawls pulled low over eyebrows, women whose age it is impossible to tell, children and old people all rush to embrace us, clinging and sobbing . . . In true Russian tradition, some search their pitiful stores in vain for a treat to offer . . .

'Our men have come!' they cry.

The joy of those faces, the happiness that lights up their eyes!

But we . . . electrified by such a reception and flushed by the on-going battle, we keep peering apprehensively over shoulders, alert for a gun barrel around the corner, for a German counter-attack. Extricating ourselves gently from clasping arms, our lines spread out and advancing in short runs from one ruined house to another, we reach the far end of what is now our village once again, clearing it of the Germans as we go.

The exhilaration of the liberators is comparable to none other. Those who have known it will agree. Those who haven't can believe me.

This is a joy that will last you for the rest of your life, till your dying day.

Most of the planes of the Red Air Force were serviced by women. Here, two engineers are loading the gun of the plane seen in the picture below.

The pilot of this plane, an 11–2 Shturmovik, Captain Sidorenko, was a former student of the Moscow Conservatoire. He spent hours decorating his plane with musical scores.

The crew of a Heinkel He III bomber surrender after being shot down. The Germans enjoyed almost undisputed supremacy in the air at the beginning of their invasion of Russia. Gradually, air superiority was won by the Red Air Force. 125,000 aircraft were produced in the Soviet Union between 1941 and 1945.

I'll never forget that day in Belorussia when we rescued 200 children. The day before, our regiment was involved in an operation to surround a major enemy force in the vicinity of Parichi. The enemy put up desperate resistance but we pushed them into a pocket and went at them with our Katyushas. That was when a farmwoman came running to our forward line. Tears streaming down her face, she said: 'Sons, come and see what those monsters have done!' We went.

In the village, by a house that had served the Nazis as field hospital, she showed us a pit that had been covered over with soil. That soil still breathed and moved. We shovelled it away and the sight of what was underneath filled us with horror. The pit was full of the bodies of little boys and girls aged between ten and twelve years. We learned that the Nazi butchers had used them to give blood transfusions to their wounded officers and then had thrown them into the pit. I sincerely wish no one ever feels what we did at that moment. The sobbing woman also told us that the retreating Nazis had taken another 200 children along with them and that she could show us in which direction they had gone. Taking her along, a group of soldiers, myself included, set out immediately by lorry. We were just in time. We managed to save the children . . .

Mine experts clear the area around Pushkin's grave, at the Sviatorgersky Monastery in Pskov province. The monastery had been occupied by the Germans who had planted special irretractable mines because they knew that the Russians would immediately want to set the grave in order. But by this time the Soviet troops knew that the retreating Germans mined everything in sight, including their own dead soldiers' bodies. The Germans' robbing, looting, burning and killing in the Pskov area was compared to the Tartar invasions.

*26th June 1944.
Explosives experts enter
the provincial capital of
Vitebsk, in Belorussia.
Before the war the city
had a population of
170,000. On the day of
liberation, only 118
people were still alive.
Most of the inhabitants
had been transported to
German concentration
camps.*

Everything's fine as usual. We've been in combat for over 10 days now but I'm safe and sound. Yes, Polya, we are nearing the happy hour of victory. If only you could realize what a historic time this is! We've left Berlin far behind already. We flanked it and are blasting the enemy where he least expected us. Our boys are really handing it to the Fritzes, they're surrendering in droves. Not all, naturally. Some of them are still snarling and snapping back like beasts and the fighting is heavy. But there's no stopping us now . . .

Well, I can't describe everything in a letter. When I return, we'll meet in Mozhga and I'll tell you all about it.

My dearest, you have been writing of your thoughts and feelings for me and asking me to believe you. Have I ever doubted you? I trust you, my precious, I trust you in all things and that is why I love you and look forward with such impatience to our meeting. That day, my dear, is not far off! I only hope I live to see it, and then we'll live happily ever after . . .

Ivan Kiryanov, the writer of this letter, was killed in action on 9th May 1945.

A Ukrainian farmer greets a Red Army tank crew entering his village with bread and salt, the foods necessary to sustain life. This was an ancient local custom for welcoming the most honoured guests. The visitor had to take a small piece of bread and dip it in the salt.

Ah, those roads . . .
Dust and fog,
Frost and fears,
And the bracken of the steppes . . .
Whether snow or wind
We'll remember, friends.
Those wartime roads
We dare never forget.
One of Marshal Zhukov's favourite songs (the others were *The Sacred War* and *Nightingales*).

Marshal Zhukov put his finger on the reason for the popularity of those songs to this very day when explaining why he liked them so much: 'Those are immortal songs because they encompass the great soul of the people.'

In a liberated village an old woman welcomes the victorious warriors with an icon, according to ancient Russian tradition. A high proportion of the Red Army came from peasant families with strong religious traditions.

A village priest blessing a column of Soviet soldiers. Many priests had been active in the partisan movement, and were honoured for their role in the war. The Church donated a great deal of money to the war effort, and endowed a tank unit called after Dmitri Donskoi, a thirteenth-century Muscovite prince whose victory over the Mongolian hordes had kept them at bay for 300 years. Dmitri was later canonized.

Tolya Frolov in the ruins of his home, in the hamlet of Ulyanova. Hundreds of thousands of Soviet children were orphaned by the war.

221

In Belorussia alone 250 villages were razed to the ground by the Germans. They would often herd the entire population into a large house or a church, and then set light to it.

Facing page: *Belorussia, 1944. This village seems to have escaped lightly. The people returning to their houses have managed to preserve quite a lot of their belongings. Elsewhere, others were less fortunate. At Zhlobin, the Germans shot 2,500 civilians during their retreat.*

After the liberation, many people had to live in dug-out shelters with their children and animals, until reconstruction could begin on a massive scale in 1946.

Ukrainian women taking home the bodies of their menfolk.

A Red Army man feeds a child whose mother has been killed by the Germans.

224

The task of tracing war orphans continues, more than 40 years later. Thousands and thousands of children were taken into orphanages when their mothers and grandmothers were killed. But in the chaos of the time it was impossible to keep records of who they were. So if their fathers returned from the army they had to hunt for their children, who might have been evacuated to any part of the Soviet Union, and possibly adopted. Every week, radio stations still broadcast details of families who were split up and are searching for each other. Newspapers also run similar campaigns from time to time.

That day I was ferrying shells to the front as usual. A battle was on but it was exceptionally quiet on the road. I got lost in thought and . . . (that's what you get for being careless) almost hit a tank which stood smack in the middle of the road with stopped engine. I opened my mouth to tell the bungling driver off but clamped it shut in a hurry. For, standing on the road was a German tank, and out of it came a smiling German officer. He calmly walked up to my lorry, opened the door and with a sweep of his hand invited me to get out and surrender. I sized up the situation. The officer was unarmed and the tank's engine was dead. My foot was on the accelerator. In the twinkling of an eye I grabbed him by the neck, pulled him to and stepped on the gas. My luck was I went forward and not back because it took the Fritzes three to four minutes to get the tank into position and start firing. That was how I arrived at the lines with the ammunition and a semi-strangled enemy officer on the footboard. The officer proved a mine of information for reconnaissance. I was awarded the Order of the Red Star . . .

Facing page: *The Germans arrive in Moscow. After these prisoners had been marched through the streets, sanitary trucks followed their route, spraying the roads with disinfectant as a final gesture of contempt.*

Despite their atrocious behaviour in Russia these German prisoners, some 57,000, were not subjected to physical attack by the Moscow crowds. Some young people booed and threw things, but they were stopped at once by their elders, who, by and large, looked on in silence. Indeed, many women were full of commiseration, and one British correspondent heard an old woman muttering, 'just like our poor boys . . . also driven to war'.

Red Army troops erect a frontier post. This poor quality photograph was taken by a soldier as his friends did the work. By September 1944, the Germans had been thrown out of all pre-1939 Soviet territory.

Victory

At the beginning of 1945 the Red Army and its allies stood ready to crush the Fascist beast in its lair'. Polish, Czechoslovak, Rumanian and Yugoslav national units, as well as the Free French 'Normandie Squadron', were now fighting alongside the Red Army. These allied units consisted of over half a million men, equipped with 16,500 guns and mortars, 1,000 tanks and self-propelled guns and over 1,600 aircraft.

The Soviet strategy involved a main thrust drive straight to Berlin. A subsidiary thrust would clear East Prussia in the north, while another would drive towards the Austrian capital, Vienna, in the south. After a terrific artillery barrage, on 12th January 1945 the Red Army began its winter offensive.

In the north, the Red Army reached the Gulf of Danzig by 26th January, cutting off the German forces in the East Prussian pocket, and containing them so that they could not break out and hinder the main thrust to Berlin. The Soviet encirclement began slowly to crush this pocket, until, one by one, Danzig, Königsberg, and other strongholds – 'strongholds' often only in Hitler's imagination – fell to the Red Army, releasing Soviet divisions for the main attack on the German capital.

To the south, in Hungary, German forces held out in Budapest throughout January. They finally capitulated on 13th February 1945. The following month the Germans mounted a counter-attack, their last of the war. But by now the forces opposing them were too strong, and after a fortnight's hard fighting the attack fell away. The road was now open to Vienna. On 29th March, the Russians crossed into Austria and on 4th April General Malinovsky's troops captured Bratislava, the capital of Germany's puppet state Slovakia, which had sent troops to fight in Russia in 1941. Nine days later, on 13th April, after a week's heavy fighting inside the city, Malinovsky's and Tolbukhin's troops took Vienna. The Russians saw Vienna as an occupied city, not an enemy one, and after the city's fall Red Army men made pilgrimages to the grave of Johann Strauss and laid wreaths on Beethoven's tomb.

The main assault on the Nazi capital was planned in two parts, one of which was to drive through Poznan in Poland and the other through Breslau on the River Oder in Germany.

The ruined city of Warsaw was liberated by the Red Army on 17th January 1945. On 26th January the Soviet forces reached Auschwitz, the most notorious of Germany's extermination camps, where hundreds of thousands had been gassed or worked to death. The camp had been evacuated and the Russians found only 2,819 invalids in the camp. A Soviet State Commission arrived and on 12th May 1945 they presented the world with their findings. The Red Army had

May 1945. A Soviet tank crew and infantry celebrate victory in front of the Brandenburg Gate.

A Soviet machine-gun crew in action in heavy fighting in Germany.

uncovered the horrors of Maidanek extermination camp, near Lublin, almost a year earlier, in July 1944. A million people, mainly Jews, had been murdered at Maidanek, two miles from the centre of Lublin. When Alexander Werth sent the BBC a detailed report on Maidanek in August 1944 executives refused to use it, thinking it unbelievable. It was not until the discovery of Belsen, Dachau and Büchenwald that people in the west were convinced of the horrors of Auschwitz and Maidanek.

By 16th April 1945 the final attack on Hitler's capital was ready to be launched. The attack started from the bridgeheads on the River Oder, and a week later on 23rd April a special communiqué stated: 'The troops of the 1st Belorussian Front, under Marshal Zhukov, launched their offensive from the bridgeheads on the Oder with the support of artillery and aircraft, and broke through the defences of Berlin. They took Frankfurt-on-the-Oder, Wannlitz, Oranienburg, Birkenwerder, Henningsdorff, Pankow, Kopenick and Karlshorst, and broke into the capital of Germany, Berlin.'

From the south, at the same time, Koniev's troops broke into the capital, taking Cottbus, Marienfelde, Teltow and other Berlin suburbs. Two days later Zhukov's and Koniev's troops met north-west of Potsdam, thereby encircling the city. On the same day, Pillau, the last German stronghold in East Prussia, was taken. On 27th April Russian and American forces met at Torgau on the Elbe, cutting the remaining German forces in two. Two days later Hitler married his mistress, Eva Braun, and committed suicide. Josef Goebbels, now Reichs-Chancellor, sent General Krebs, formerly the Military Attaché in Moscow, to Marshal Chuikov in order to ascertain the terms that would be acceptable to the Russians. Hearing that unconditional surrender was the only formula that Russia and her allies would consider, Goebbels and Krebs committed suicide on 1st May. The following day the city surrendered. A week later Germany followed suit.

On 9th May 1945 it was all over. At ten past one in the morning the voice of Radio Moscow's chief announcer, Yuri Levitan, announced: 'Attention, this is Moscow. Germany has capitulated . . . this day, in honour of the victorious Great Patriotic War, is to be a national holiday, a festival of victory.' Stalin spoke briefly to the jubilant crowds at 10 pm: 'My dear fellow countrymen and women. I am proud today to call you my comrades. Your courage has defeated the Nazis. The war is over. . . . Now we shall build a Russia fit for heroes and heroines.' It was, as the Manchester *Guardian* correspondent said, 'the greatest moment in this country's history since the Revolution.'

Of the Axis powers, only Japan remained. On 8th August, the Soviet Union, under terms agreed at the Yalta conference, declared war on Japan. The allies, led by the USA, had already advanced to the threshold and had subjected Japan to heavy bombing by long-range aircraft. An eleven-day war in Manchuria began. The one big battle of this campaign was fought near Ningtu, roughly midway between Vladivostock and Kirin, around a railway junction and the valleys and hills to the north of the town. The Japanese Kwangtung Army (31 infantry divisions and two tank brigades) was still resisting strongly when news of their country's capitulation broke, after the dropping of atom bombs on Hiroshima and Nagasaki by the USA. Japan formally surrendered on 14th August, but the news did not at once reach Manchuria, where the fighting continued until 19th August. 600,000 Soviet troops in 80 infantry divisions and four armoured corps took part in the campaign, with 1,000 tanks and 3,000 planes.

The process of demobilization began as soon as the war was over. At the end of the war in Europe there were almost eleven million men in the Red Army. By February 1946 there were only about five million. The first to be demobbed were those who had worked in industry or agriculture.

The task of reconstruction lay ahead.

At the end of June it was decided to start bringing the troops home. The first of them were back in Russia in July, when this photograph was taken at the Belorussia station in Moscow.

At the end of hostilities, the Red Army consisted of something like 510 Infantry Divisions and Brigades, 34 Cavalry Divisions, 40 Artillery Divisions, 25 tank corps, 13 mechanized corps, 60 tank brigades, 180 tank regiments, 150 artillery regiments, 125 air divisions of the Red Air Force, plus supply and transport troops – in all, not far short of 11 million men. Demobilization reduced this figure to 5 million by February 1946.

On 13th April 1945, after a week's heavy fighting, the Red Army occupied Vienna. Here, Soviet troops are seen driving past the Houses of Parliament on the Franzensring, towing a heavy Hauser gun.

On 16th April 1945, the final Russian offensive against Berlin started. The Red Army reached the capital on 23rd April. A week later, Hitler committed suicide and on 2nd May the city surrendered to the Red Army.

Here, Soviet troops celebrate the fall of the city in the Tiergarten.

Soldiers of the 2nd Belorussian Front were the first to cross the Oder on the way to Berlin, using boats and rafts. Here, military hardware crosses the river by pontoon bridge. Marshal Koniev forced the Oder along a wide front in Silesia and isolated Breslau on 6th February 1945.

We sailed on the morning of 10th January 1945. About a day later we reached the point of submersion and signalled our thanks to our escort. Now for the plunge! The sealed envelope with orders is opened. We are to proceed to Danzig Gulf. Our target – big-tonnage enemy warships and transports.

It is sixteen days since we started on our hunt. We've had to evade enemy planes, submarines and anti-submarine boats many times by submerging or plunging to greater depths. But our quarry evaded us. Finally, on 30th January, at about 21:00 hours, Petty Officer 2nd Class Anatolii Vinogradov, who was standing watch in the signal room, sighted several white lights.

After a two-hour chase our submarine got ready for battle. The order from the bridge came – forward torpedo tube, fire!

Our vessel veered and went down, but we did not escape pursuit. We detected four enemy destroyers and three patrol boats. The chase was on.

Shallow water prevented us from submerging deeper. We were forced to dodge attacks and to manoeuvre fifteen metres below surface. The slightest inaccuracy could lead to disaster. Further down we could be blown up by depth charges, closer to the surface we risked ramming. The pursuit continued for more than four hours. In the meantime, a radiogram from headquarters advised us that the S-13 submarine had sunk the *Wilhelm Güstloff*, displacement over 25,000 tons. Some 8,000 SS, SD and Gestapo officers and men plus 3,700 enemy submariners went down with it.

Russian and American troops meet at Torgau on the Elbe, 27th April 1945.

Valentina Tokaryeva was a medical orderly. Her story is a good illustration of what the last kilometres over enemy territory cost.

'. . . We were ordered to take Glagau. After the artillery had softened up the enemy lines, our commander ordered the company to attack. The soldiers climbed out of the trenches, rose and then dropped flat on the ground again under the massed fire. Apparently, the artillery hadn't fully suppressed the enemy batteries. Twice the officer ordered the company to attack and failed both times. That was when I thought: the officer is one thing, but what if I, a girl, get up and dash forward? The men will be sure to follow. I felt as though something pushed me up from the ground. I jumped out of the trench, the bullets whistling all around me, and ran forward shouting: Hurrah! Forward! Follow me!

I noticed the company was keeping abreast, some were even overtaking me . . . That's how we broke into the enemy trenches.'

After the liberation of Berlin the First Ukrainian Front, under Marshal Koniev, carried on to Prague. The troops reached the city on 9th May 1945. Koniev's arrival prevented destruction of the city, as the Czech Resistance battled with the Germans.

Some of the people of Belgrade welcome the Soviet troops under Marshal Tolbukhin. Together with Marshal Tito's partisans, they liberated the capital on 20th October 1944.

Jubilant Soviet soldiers capture a bunker on the eastern side of Berlin. The entire city was surrounded by fortifications, but in this sector they had been badly damaged by artillery fire.

Facing page: IL–2 assault planes over Berlin.

Loading a Katyusha rocket launcher to fire at the Reichstag.

A rocket on the Katyusha which is inscribed 'To the Reichstag'.

Soviet 'Josef Stalin' tanks on the streets of Berlin.

Berliners surrender, despite the threat by Dr Goebbels, the City's Gauleiter and Defence Commissioner, that he would have streets blown up that displayed the white flag.

Russian soldiers on the streets of Berlin. Behind them a notice, neatly chalked on the wall, reads 'Berlin remains German' – one of Dr Goebbels' last propaganda slogans.

Our field hospital was assigned the duty of treating and looking after the former inmates of Auschwitz – a death camp the name of which has come to symbolize Nazi barbarity. When we, the other doctors and nurses and I, entered this place of horror with its 17,000 surviving inmates, we saw piles of corpses which the retreating enemy had not had time to dispose of. The furnaces of the crematorium were still warm. But more terrifying than the corpses was the appearance of those the Nazis had not had time to torture to death, to hang, bury or burn. Those people were emaciated in the extreme. Adults and children, men and women, they all looked exactly alike in face and body and were incapable of moving about on their own. In the children's eyes – this is something I'll never forget – was an unchildlike, no, not an unchildlike, an inhuman terror of people they didn't know. For almost a month, in impossible conditions, we sanitized and treated the former prisoners. We worked round the clock. They had to be fed from a spoon, held up to be washed, they had to be combed as they could do none of those things themselves. Finally, there came a day, a very happy day, when some of them were well enough to venture out of the barracks into the warm spring sunshine. At last, I saw the children smiling for the first time and I understood that life was indestructible, that it was beyond fascists of any stripe to stamp it out.

The Volkssturm, Hitler's last hope. In September 1944 the Führer decreed the establishment of this Home Guard, consisting of Hitler Youth and men who were too old or unfit for active service. Their military value was negligible.

As Europe was liberated from German rule by the Russian, British and American armies, unimaginable horrors were uncovered. Russian troops were the first to arrive at Auschwitz, one of the most notorious Nazi extermination camps, on 26th January 1945. They found 2,819 invalids, left behind by the Nazis. They were nursed back to health by the Russians. It is impossible to calculate how many Slavs, Jews, gypsies and others were gassed and burnt in Auschwitz and its satellite camps, but it is certainly not much less than one million.

The Commandant of Berlin, General Karl Weidling, comes out of his bunker to surrender, 2nd May 1945.

Georgi Zhukov receiving the German surrender on behalf of the Soviet Union.

242

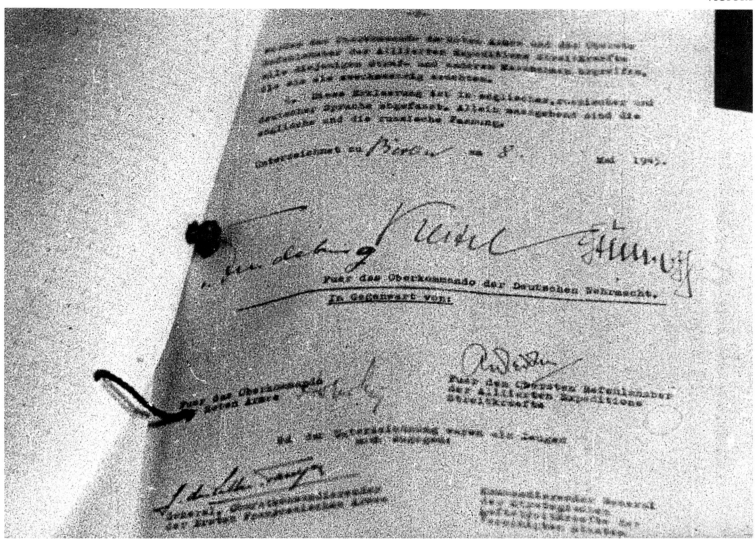

Field Marshal Keitel signed the German surrender with the Act of Capitulation.

The last epic Berlin operation was launched at 05.00 hours on 16th April. On the first day alone 42,000 artillery pieces and mortars fired 2,450 freight-car loads of shells into the enemy lines!

In his book *Reminiscences and Thoughts* this is how Marshal G. Zhukov describes the impact on him of the first minutes of the closing battle of World War II:

'Thousands of multicoloured rockets flew into the air. At the signal, 140 searchlights, stationed at every 200 metres, were turned on. The field of battle was flooded by light, blinding the enemy and spotlighting the targets for our attacking tanks and infantry. It was an impressive sight. I don't remember anything in my life to rival the sensation.'

The end of the Third Reich. A German NCO prisoner outside the ruins of the Reichstag.

Facing page: *Planting the Red Flag on the Reichstag, 1.45 pm, 30th April 1945. Viktor Temin, one of the outstanding Soviet war photographers, managed to persuade Marshal Zhukov to let him photograph it from the air. He then flew the plane, without permission, to Moscow so that his pictures of the event would be published before anyone else's. The next day he returned to Berlin with an armful of copies of* Pravda, *with his photographs on the front page.*

*9th May 1945. Victory
celebrations in Red
Square.*

Marshal Koniev with officers of his First Ukrainian Front at the victory parade.

At the end of the victory parade, German banners are thrown down by Russian soldiers on the steps of the Lenin Mausoleum. Veterans of the parade recall that it rained hard all morning, while the parade was taking place.

Facing page: *Arriving home.*

Back home.

That evening, there was the biggest firework display ever held in Moscow.

The Second World War

EVENTS IN THE SOVIET UNION	EVENTS ELSEWHERE
1939	
	1 September Germany invades Poland *3 September* Britain and France declare war on Germany
1940 *12 March* Soviet-Finnish Treaty signed	
	14 May Germany invades France *10 June* Italy declares war on Britain and France *14 June* Germans enter Paris *July–October* Battle of Britain
1941	*6 April* Germans invade Greece and Yugoslavia
22 June Germany invades Soviet Union *28 June* Germans capture Minsk and large parts of Lithuania, Latvia and Ukraine *16 July* Germans reach Smolensk *8 September* Germans capture Schlusselburg, completing the blockade of Leningrad *30 September* German offensive against Moscow begins *30 October* Nine-month siege of Sebastopol begins	

EVENTS IN THE SOVIET UNION	EVENTS ELSEWHERE
	12 November HMS *Ark Royal* sunk *18 November* British offensive in the Western desert begins
6 December Russian counter- offensive at Moscow begins	
	7 December Japanese bomb Pearl Harbor and raid Malaya *8 December* Britain and USA declare war on Japan *11 December* Hitler declares war on USA
15 December Russians recapture Klin and Istra	
1942	
	15 February Singapore surrenders *30 May* Thousand-bomber raid on Cologne *3 June* Battle of Midway begins
3 July Fall of Sebastopol	
	19 August Dieppe raid
13 September German attack on Stalingrad intensifies	
	23 October Battle of El Alamein begins *13 November* Sea battle of Guadalcanal
19 November Russian counter- offensive at Stalingrad begins	

EVENTS IN THE SOVIET UNION	EVENTS ELSEWHERE	EVENTS IN THE SOVIET UNION	EVENTS ELSEWHERE

1943

23 January
Eighth Army reaches
Tripoli

31 January
Paulus surrenders at
Stalingrad

20 April
Massacre in the Warsaw
Ghetto

5 July
Battle of Kursk begins

10 July
Allies land in Sicily

5 August
Russians take Orel and
Belgorod

3 September
Allies invade Italy

6 November
Russians recapture Kiev

28 November
Tehran conference begins
26 December
Scharnhorst sunk

1944
27 January
Leningrad completely
relieved
4 March
Russian spring offensive
opens in the Ukraine
9 May
Sebastopol taken

13 June
First V1 bomb on London
15 June
First Super-Fortress raid
on Japan
25 August
Paris liberated
17 September
Battle of Arnhem begins
29 September
Russians enter Yugoslavia

1945
4 February
Yalta conference opens

1 April
Americans invade
Okinawa
12 April
Death of President
Roosevelt
13 April
Russians take Vienna
25 April
American and Russian
forces meet on the Elbe
30 April
Hitler's suicide
2 May
Berlin surrenders to the
Russians
7 May
Jodl signs unconditional
surrender at Eisenhower's
HQ at Reims
8 May
'VE' Day. Keitel signs
surrender at Zhukov's
HQ near Berlin
9 May
Victory Day in the
Soviet Union

9 May
Russians take Prague

6 August
Atom bomb dropped on
Hiroshima

8 August
Soviet Union declares
war on Japan

9 August
Atom bomb dropped on
Nagasaki
2 September
Japan signs Act of
Capitulation on board
USS *Missouri*

Index

(Page numbers in italics refer to captions)